Ellis and Kevan
on
Credit Hire

Aidan Ellis Barrister,
Middle Temple, MA (Hons)(Cantab) LLM

and

Tim Kevan Barrister (non-practising),
Middle Temple, MA (Hons)(Cantab)

Law Brief Publishing

Published 2016 by
Law Brief Publishing
30 The Parks
Minehead
Somerset
TA24 8BT

www.lawbriefpublishing.com

Paperback: 978-1-911035-07-7

To

Imogen and Thea

and

Louise, Grace and Hope

Contents

Acknowledgements

We are grateful for the support of our colleagues and former colleagues in Chambers at Temple Garden Chambers. In particular to Dean Norton, Dominic Adamson, Paul McGrath, Jonathan Hough, Marcus Grant and Tim Sharpe among others. We are also grateful to our wives Imogen Ellis and Louise Kevan for their love and support.

Type of Vehicle - Pg 83

INTRODUCTION

The death of credit hire litigation has often been predicted. After each new higher court case, there is a tendency to imagine that all issues have been conclusively resolved, facilitating the negotiated settlement of the majority of cases. And yet credit hire litigation continues. Indeed it prospers, to the concern of many County Court Judges. It is no exaggeration to say that credit hire cases, often on similar issues in low value cases, come before the courts every day. Partly, this is due to the relentless tide of new statutory instruments affecting consumer credit. Partly, it is simply because many of the issues that arise turn on the facts of individual cases.

Many credit hire cases originate in very similar facts. The Defendant negligently causes a road traffic accident in which the Claimant's vehicle is damaged. Whilst the Claimant's own vehicle is off the road being repaired (or replaced), the Claimant may want to be able to use an alternative vehicle. One option for the Claimant is to obtain a replacement vehicle from a credit hire company.

It is easy to see why credit hire is attractive to the Claimant. Primarily, it avoids the Claimant having to pay for the hire up front; indeed the Claimant can simply seek to recover the cost of the credit hire from the Defendant. The credit hire company can also provide accident management services, assisting the Claimant for example by supervising the repair process.

On the other hand, Defendant Insurers will be concerned about the high costs of the resulting credit hire charges, which they regularly list amongst the factors driving up car insurance premiums.

The result is frequently litigation, in which the Claimant, supported by the credit hire company, seeks to recover the credit hire charges from the Defendant and the Defendant, through the Defendant's Insurer, seeks to eliminate or reduce them. Thus although many cases are fought in the name of the individual drivers, the real battle is fought between the credit hire companies and the insurers. This book is intended as a guide to the issues which arise in the course of that litigation.

This book is aimed at anyone who has any involvement with the credit hire industry from garages and credit hire company employees to insurance claims handlers, solicitors and barristers. So, too, perhaps at those litigants curious enough to want to find out about the battle in which they have innocently become involved following a road traffic accident. It is hoped that it will offer assistance both to those tackling the subject for the first time and to those experienced in its most intricate details.

Since the last edition, there have been a number of important developments. In particular, the Court of Appeal has been active in this area, delivering decisions affecting basic hire rates, impecuniosity and mitigation.

We have kept the structure of the previous edition. The first three chapters address the main contemporary issues: rates, impecuniosity and mitigation. We will then turn to deal with the enforceability of credit hire agreements. In recent years, the focus here has shifted away from the old arguments based on the Consumer Credit Act 1974 and onto compliance with newer statutory instruments. Whilst it remains important to appreciate the background of the Consumer Credit Act litigation, we will look in particular at the flurry of litigation generated by the Cancellation of Contracts made in a Consumer's Home or Place of Work Regulations 2008 and the possible impact of the Consumer Credit (EU Directive) Regulations 2010.

The law is stated as it is understood by the authors in October 2016. Any errors are the authors' own for which we apologise. The purpose of this book is to highlight the various areas of law potentially associated with credit hire. It is not intended to be a substitute for legal advice and readers researching a particular problem or particular case should not rely upon its contents in isolation but should instead refer to textbooks on the particular aspect of the problem and to legally qualified professionals. Nor have we been able to cover every one of the many first instance decisions on credit hire cases, though we have tried to refer to those which raise interesting points.

CHAPTER ONE
RATES

A. **INTRODUCTION**

> *"the major protection for the defendant and his insurers is that the claimant can only recover the 'spot' or market rate of hire"*

So spoke the Court of Appeal in *Copley v Lawn*[1] in considering the proper scope of arguments relating to mitigation of loss in credit hire cases. As set out below, subsequent cases suggest a greater role for mitigation in credit hire cases than the Court of Appeal allowed in *Copley*. But far less contentious was the Court's identification of the market rate of hire as the 'major protection' for the defendant in current credit hire cases. It is no exaggeration to say that the County Courts are still grappling with credit hire cases in which the daily rate is the main issue on a daily basis. The determination of the market rate of hire remains highly contentious and deserves its place in the first chapter of this revised edition.

Disputes over the rate of hire reflect a fundamental dispute between the insurance and credit hire industries. Insurers have long complained that credit hire rates cost substantially more than the equivalent market rates. But the method of determining the 'equivalent' market rate has

---

1 [2009] EWCA Civ 580 at para. 6.

always been controversial. Moreover, credit hire companies argue that they provide a different service – for example, providing hire vehicles on favourable insurance terms – which is not matched by ordinary hire companies or which, if ordinary hire companies could match it, would cost no less than the credit hire rate.

The present position, frequently restated in the leading cases, is that an ordinary claimant is not entitled to recover the full credit hire rate because it is said to incorporate irrecoverable benefits additional to the provision of a vehicle. As a result, only the equivalent market hire rate is recoverable. We will consider the exception which arises in relation to impecunious claimants in the next chapter. In this chapter, we will consider the authorities for this general principle and the reasoning behind it. We will then go on to consider how the Court should determine the equivalent market hire rate by considering the leading authorities and the evidential issues which commonly arise.

As explained below, the additional benefits issue is separate from arguments about reasonableness and mitigation. The distinct arguments that may arise about reasonableness in relation to rates are addressed in Chapter Three.

B. CREDIT HIRE RATE OR BASIC HIRE RATE?

It is perhaps helpful to start by stating the general rule again. In *Dimond v Lovell*,[2] after emerging from the thicket of consumer credit issues to address the issue of rates, Lord Hoffmann (with whom Lord Browne-Wilkinson agreed) stated that:-

> *"in the case of a hiring from an accident hire company, the equivalent spot rate will ordinarily be the net loss after allowance has been made for the additional benefits which the accident hire company has provided."*

It should be acknowledged at the outset that this part of the speech was *obiter dicta*. The *ratio* of *Dimond v Lovell* related to the enforceability of

---

2   *Dimond v Lovell* [2002] 1 AC 384.

the hire agreement under the Consumer Credit Act 1974. This led Lord Saville to abstain from deciding the issue on the basis that it:-

> "*does not arise for decision in the present case. This is a question of great importance and difficulty, the answer to which may well have widespread ramifications. It is accordingly a question that I would prefer to consider in a case where it does arise for decision.*"

Although the other four Judges did address the issue, Lord Nicholls dissented on the basis that the full credit hire rate should be recoverable and Lord Hobhouse agreed that the credit hire rate should not be recoverable, but proposed a different way of ascertaining the recoverable damages. Only Lord Browne-Wilkinson agreed entirely with Lord Hoffmann.

Nevertheless it would, in practice, be very difficult to argue that lower courts should not follow Lord Hoffmann's approach. As the Court of Appeal explained in *Sayce v TNT*:

> "*There are circumstances in which, although not technically bound by a decision of a higher court, a lower court should follow and apply that decision, even though it may disagree with it. There may be room for legitimate disagreement between judges of co-ordinate jurisdiction and in those circumstances reasoned difference of opinion may provide a useful springboard for an appeal. That is not the case, however, where a higher court has decided a question of principle, albeit obiter, for the purpose of clarifying the law for the profession at large. It would not be right, for example, for this court to disregard those parts of their Lordships' speeches in Dimond v Lovell that deal with the recovery of that part of the credit hire costs that relate to additional benefits on the grounds that they are obiter*"[3]

Moreover, many subsequent cases confirm that Lord Hoffmann's *dicta* have become firmly entrenched in the jurisprudence. They have been repeatedly confirmed in subsequent cases. Thus in *Burdis v Livsey*, the

---

3 *Sayce v TNT* [2011] EWCA Civ 1583 paragraph 24.

Court of Appeal endeavoured to follow the House of Lords' *"guidance as to the principles to be applied in arriving at the correct measure of damages for loss of use".*[4]

In a similar vein in *Bee v Jenson*, the Court of Appeal noted that *"the House held, secondly, that even if the claimant could have recovered he could have recovered no more than the spot charge and not the charges made for an agreement that entitled the claimant to more benefit than the cost of hire itself".*[5]

In *Copley v Lawn*, the Court of Appeal *"regarded it as well settled that, although a claimant can recover the cost of hiring a replacement car, he can only recover the reasonable rate of such hire; that has been held in Dimond v Lovell to be the market or spot rate".*[6]

In *Bent v (1) Highways and Utilities Construction Ltd (2) Allianz Insurance*[7] ("Bent no1"), the Court of Appeal summarised the authorities thus *"The authorities establish that in the case of "pecunious" (as the Judge described Mr Bent) claimants, the damages to be awarded are normally to be assessed at "spot hire" rates – the rate at which a broadly similar car could be had on the market."*

In *Bent v (1) Highways and Utilities Construction Ltd (2) Allianz Insurance no2* ("Bent no2"), the Court of Appeal repeated *"If the claimant could afford to hire a replacement car in the normal way, ie. without credit terms and by paying in advance,*[8] *then the damages recoverable for loss of use of the damaged car will be that sum which is attributable to the basic hire rate of the replacement car".*[9]

---

4 *Burdis v Livsey* [2003] QB 36 paragraph 136.

5 *Bee v Jenson* (2007) 4 All ER 791 para. 6.

6 *Copley v Lawn* para. 3.

7 [2010] EWCA Civ 292, see para. 6 in particular.

8 Note that this does not exactly encapsulate the definition of impecuniosity offered by the House of Lords in *Lagden v O'Connor*, which will be explored in more detail in the next chapter.

9 [2011] EWCA Civ 1384.

The result is that, although it was strictly *obiter*, the general rule established by Lord Hoffmann in *Dimond* is now deeply entrenched in the jurisprudence. Unless the issue returns to the Supreme Court (and unless the claimant is impecunious) the general rule is therefore that the claimant is restricted to recovering "the equivalent spot hire rate".

The Reason for the General Rule

Before going on to consider how the Court should determine the basic hire rate, it is necessary to explain the reason for this general rule. Understanding the reason for the rule, should guide the application of the rule to the evidence.

I n *Dimond*, Lord Hoffmann, with whom Lord Browne Wilkinson agreed, stated:

> *"My Lords, I would accept the judge's finding that Mrs. Dimond acted reasonably in going to 1st Automotive and availing herself of its services . . . She cannot therefore be said not to have taken reasonable steps to mitigate her damage.*
>
> *But that does not necessarily mean that she can recover the full amount charged by 1st Automotive. By virtue of her contract, she obtained not only the use of the car but additional benefits as well."*

This finding is significant because by accepting that Mrs Dimond acted reasonably in going to the credit hire company, as the Court of Appeal and the trial Judge had already held below, Lord Hoffmann made it clear that the reason for not allowing the claimant to recover the credit hire rate is nothing to do with mitigation or reasonableness. Rather it is a matter of betterment.

The point is that a credit hire company typically provides a range of accident management services to a claimant, which go beyond the simple provision of a replacement vehicle. Lord Hoffmann identified the additional benefits inherent in the credit hire contract at page 401 as:

i. the credit charge itself

    "She was relieved of the necessity of laying out the money to pay for the car."

ii. the costs of the action

    "She was relieved of the risk of having to bear the irrecoverable costs of successful litigation and the risk, small though it might be, of having to bear the expense of unsuccessful litigation". Lord Hoffmann also referred to other associated costs: "Paying commission to brokers"; "checking that the accident was not the hirer's fault."

iii. possibly avoiding a residual liability

    "Depending upon the view one takes of the terms of agreement, she may have been relieved of the possibility of having to pay for the car at all."

iv. relieving the anxiety of the claim

    "She was relieved of the trouble and anxiety of pursuing a claim against Mr. Lovell or the C.I.S."

Lord Hoffmann continued:-

"My Lords, English law does not regard the need for any of these additional services as compensatable loss. As Sir Richard Scott V.-C. said (at [1999] 3 W.L.R. 561, 580) "damages for worry and for the nuisance caused by having to deal with the consequences of an accident are not recoverable." If Mrs. Dimond had borrowed the hire money, paid someone else to conduct the claim on her behalf and insured herself against the risk of losing and any irrecoverable costs, her expenses would not have been recoverable. But the effect of the award of damages is that Mrs. Dimond has obtained compensation for them indirectly because they were offered as part of a package by 1st Automotive. There is in my opinion something wrong with this conclusion."

He then referred to the cases of *British Westinghouse Electric and Manufacturing Co. Ltd. v. Underground Electric Railways Co. of London Ltd* [1912] A.C. 673 and *Bellingham v. Dhillon* [1973] Q.B. 304 which emphasised that only compensatory damages were recoverable. In other words, additional benefits received whilst mitigating loss should not be taken into account in quantifying the claim. But how does this impact on the assessment of damages? Lord Hoffmann explained:-

> *"How does one calculate the additional benefits that Mrs. Dimond received by choosing the 1st Automotive package to mitigate the loss caused by the accident to her car? . . . I do not think that a court can ignore the fact that, one way or another, the other benefits have to be paid for . . . How does one estimate the value of these additional benefits that Mrs. Dimond obtains? It seems to me that prima facie their value is represented by the difference between what she was willing to pay 1ˢᵗ Automotive and what she would have been willing to pay an ordinary car hire company for the use of a car . . . I quite accept that a determination of the value of the benefits which must be brought into account will depend upon the facts of each case. But the principle to be applied is that in the British Westinghouse case [1912] A.C. 673 and this seems to me to lead to the conclusion that in the case of hiring from an accident hire company the equivalent spot rate will ordinarily be the net loss..."*

Thus, the only way to strip out the additional and irrecoverable benefits from the credit hire charges is by reference to the "equivalent spot rate".

On the face of it, Lord Hobhouse adopted a similar analysis. He expressly said that he agreed with Lord Hoffmann that the judge and the majority of the Court of Appeal had approached the issue in the wrong way. He also decided that Mrs Dimond had acted reasonably and went on to emphasise the additional benefits contained in the credit hire contract. He described these at pages 406 - 407 as:

i.   the credit charge itself

> "It is financing the transaction until the expected recovery is made from the other party".

ii.   the costs of the action

"it is bearing the cost of handling the claim and effecting that recovery"; "something in respect of costs".

iii.   possibly avoiding a residual liability

"it is bearing a commercial (though not normally the legal) risk that there may be a failure to make that recovery".

Thus aside from one (removing the anxiety of litigation), Lord Hobhouse identified the same additional benefits as Lord Hoffmann.

However, his analysis of how the recoverable damages should be calculated differed from that of Lord Hoffmann. Lord Hobhouse favoured *"the approach of making a commercial apportionment between the cost of hiring a car and the cost of the other benefits included in the scheme."*

He explained that Mrs Dimond would not have been able to recover the whole cost of the credit hire charges *"as the cost of mitigating the loss of use of her car"*. He said later, *"The elements to which the uplift in the charges of the accident hire company was attributable were (and inevitably must be) elements which were not properly included in the claim for damages for loss of use."*

In other words, the claim for the uplift was not recoverable in the claim for loss of use. This may have left open the possibility that it may be recoverable in other ways. Indeed, this is supported by his further statement that *"As appears from what I have said, some might be recovered from the wrongdoer in another form"*. In practice, however, it is difficult to see how the Claimant could recover for these additional benefits via any other route. First, the Claimant would not be able to recover for the same thing twice:

"The necessity to make some apportionment or other reduction in the claim is demonstrated by the need to avoid double counting. Prima facie, the court should award statutory interest on the claim; but

here the claim already included some element of interest. Similarly the claim included something in respect of costs; to award costs as well would involve some duplication."

Second, Lord Hobhouse stated that, *"it is unlikely that any scheme could be devised which would enable the insurance element to be recovered"*. This appears to refer to the additional benefit which comprised the possibility of avoiding a residual liability.

The heart of the difference between Lord Hoffmann and Lord Hobhouse is this: Lord Hoffmann thought that the measure of the Claimant's recoverable loss could safely be approximated by looking to the equivalent spot hire rate while Lord Hobhouse seemed to prefer an approach based on stripping out the unrecoverable additional benefits from the credit hire charges.

As the caselaw set out above and below illustrates, it is Lord Hoffmann's approach – searching for the basic hire rate - which is most often adopted in practice. However, that does not mean that the Courts have not expressed certain reservations. From time to time, the Court of Appeal has flirted with the idea that the credit hire company could disclose details of its charging structure in order to allow the charge for credit to be stripped out in a manner reminiscent of Lord Hobhouse's approach. Most recently, in *Stevens v Equity Syndicate Management Ltd* the Court of Appeal canvassed "whether credit hire companies could, as a matter of course, disclose their estimate of the BHR alongside every quoted credit hire rate".[10] It later suggested that the selection of the lowest reasonable rate was justified because "the credit hire company is in the best position to elaborate upon and give disclosure relating to its charging structures".[11]

On the whole, however, the Courts have retreated from the disclosure and costs implications of any attempt to strip out the elements of the credit rate.[12] Nevertheless, it remains open to credit hire companies to

---

10 *Para.* 30.

11 *Para.* 36.

12 *Para.* 30.

seek to avoid the analysis of basic hire rates altogether by providing appropriate disclosure of their charging structures and an analysis breaking down the credit hire charges into their constituent elements.

For completeness, in dissent in *Dimond* Lord Nicholls accepted that the credit hire contract incorporated additional benefits but argued that the uplift should be recoverable. He identified the same "additional services" as Lord Hobhouse:

i. the credit charge itself

   "The hirer does not have to produce any money . . . at the time of the hiring".

ii. the costs of the action

   "The hire company pursues the allegedly negligent driver's insurers"; "The hire company is not deterred by having to bring court proceedings should this become necessary".

iii. possibly avoiding a residual liability

   "The hirer does not have to produce any money, either at the time of the hiring or at all"; "If the claim is unsuccessful, in practice the hire company does not pursue the hirer".

Lord Nicholls then went on to explain why these additional benefits ought, in his view, to be recoverable:-

"The additional services . . . redress the imbalance between the individual car owner and the insurance companies. They enable car owners to shift from themselves to the insurance companies a loss which properly belongs to the insurers but which, in practice, owners of cars often have to bear themselves. So long as the charge for the additional services is reasonable, this charge should be part of the recoverable damages.

A measure of damages which does not achieve this result would be sadly deficient. The law on the measure of damages should reflect the practicalities of the situation in which a wronged person finds himself. Otherwise it would mean that the law's response to a wrong is a right to damages which will often be illusory in practice. I do not believe this can be the present state of the law in a situation which affects thousands of people every year."

However, Lord Nicholls' was a lone voice in dissent. As set out above, the majority approach in *Dimond* is now firmly entrenched in the jurisprudence. His dissent is now mainly interesting from a historical perspective.

C. DETERMINING THE BASIC HIRE RATE

Identifying that the equivalent spot hire rate will ordinarily be the amount of recoverable damages, as the House of Lords did in *Dimond*, is helpful as a general principle. But it does not guide the County Courts in determining what the equivalent spot hire rate is in specific cases. This issue has been addressed by the Court of Appeal on no fewer than four occasions. Each decision favours a different approach. We will set out each decision in detail before attempting to draw some conclusions.

a) Burdis v Livsey

In the first case, *Burdis v Livsey,* the Court of Appeal began by identifying the difficulty of the task. They pointed out that hire rates are "in constant flux". This is no doubt correct: they vary depending on the season and depending on the availability of particular vehicles. Furthermore the rates charged by different companies may vary considerably. Thus there is no single market rate as such.

At first instance in *Burdis*, the Judge had considered a number of ways of arriving at the right measure of damages:-

1. Analysing the charges made by the credit hire company to uncover which charges related to irrecoverable additional benefits and which simply related to hiring the car. Note that this appears to be the approach that Lord Hobhouse in *Dimond* had preferred. But both the Judge and the Court of Appeal considered that this approach was too *"cumbersome"* to apply. It would lead to disproportionate costs and lengthy disclosure exercises.

2. Applying an arbitrary *"reasonable discount"* to the credit hire charges. The Court of Appeal also dismissed this approach, *"we do not believe it appropriate in the absence of agreement between the parties or without cogent evidence as to what the discount should be. Further, as the judge pointed out, once the courts start applying a particular discount the total charge may be increased."*

3. Considering the actual hire rates locally. This creates its own difficulties such as what companies to survey and whether to take the highest or the lowest rate. With some modifications as to the detail, this was the route which was eventually approved.

4. The approach that the Judge in fact adopted was based on expert evidence given by Mr Mainz on behalf of the Insurers. Mr Mainz had carried out a survey of car hire rates including those charged by the best known national hire companies and a random selection of smaller companies. His figures thus provided a band of rates, which were a snapshot of the hire market as at January 2001.[13] The Judge decided to award an average based on the Mainz report. He then applied a 10% uplift to the average of these rates, to take account of the fact that the survey was carried out in January whereas the actual hire was in peak season.

---

13 In *Burdis v Livsey*, the Court of Appeal heard five appeals together. The Court used one set of illustrative facts as the basis for its decision, which were drawn from *Sen v Steelform Engineering Co Ltd*. Dr Sen the claimant in that case had hired a car for three days from 3 – 5 June 1999.

The Court of Appeal rejected this approach. They held:

> *"146 ...That cannot be right. A person who needs to hire a car because of the negligence of another must, subject to mitigating his loss, be entitled to recover the actual cost of hire not an average derived from the Mainz report. If the principle adopted by the judge is correct then it would seem appropriate also to apply that principle to the cost of car repair, namely a claimant may only recover the average of the charges of garages. But a person whose car is damaged should in appropriate circumstances recover the cost to him of repair and loss of use. His recovery should not be restricted to an average of car repair or hire rates nor should he be able to recover that average cost if the actual cost is less. We believe that the solution is to apply normal legal principles.*

The Court of Appeal also expressly accepted the criticisms advanced by the claimant that (1) the claimant should be entitled to recover the true cost of hire not simply an average (2) the uplift of 10% was arbitrary and (3) the adoption of the Mainz report was not a "cheap and workable" solution since the Mainz report would not be admissible or applicable in the mass of other cases which were pending.

The Court of Appeal then set out the correct approach to take. This section of the judgment is crucial and so is set out in full below.

> *147. The fundamental principle is that a person whose car has been damaged is entitled to compensation for the loss caused. In a case where such loss includes loss of use and he establishes a need for a replacement, he is entitled to the cost of hiring a replacement car. He can go round to the nearest car hire company and is prima facie entitled to recover the amount charged whether or not the charge is at the top of the range of car hire rates. However the basic principle is qualified by the duty to take reasonable steps to mitigate the loss. What is reasonable will depend on the particular circumstances.*

> *148. We do not anticipate that the application of the correct legal*
> *principles will lead to disproportionate costs in small cases. The*
> *claim will be based on evidence as to the rate charged by a car hire*
> *company in the relevant area. Perhaps the rate will be at the top*
> *end of the range of company rates. Thereafter the evidential burden*
> *passes to the insurers to show that it would not have been reasonable*
> *to use that particular car hire company and that the reasonable*
> *course would be to use another company which charged a lower*
> *rate. What is reasonable and whether a loss is avoidable are ques-*
> *tions of fact, not law, which District and County Court judges*
> *regularly decide. It can arise in many different types of cases,*
> *ranging from damage to chattels to a failure to take action. We do*
> *not believe that a decision on such issues in respect of car hire*
> *charges will be any more difficult than in respect of car repair*
> *charges."*

We will return to try to reconcile this passage with the later Court of Appeal decisions. But it is worth making one observation on terminology at this stage. In its decision, the Court of Appeal consistently refers to credit hire companies as "accident hire companies". The reference in paragraph 148 to a "car hire company" must therefore be to a spot hire company. But if this is correct, then the Defendant might argue that the Court of Appeal was placing the burden of proof on the Claimant, at least initially, to provide evidence of spot hire rates. This is supported by the Court of Appeal continuing that "thereafter the evidential burden passes to the insurers". In order for the burden to pass to the insurers "thereafter", it must have been on the Claimant initially. As set out below, however, subsequent cases make it clear that the burden of proof rests on the Defendant to show that the equivalent spot hire rate was lower than the credit hire rate.

b) Bent no1

In the first appeal in the Bent case, the trial Judge had rejected the evidence of spot hire rates tendered by the Defendant primarily on the basis that it was evidence of comparable rates in 2009 when the hire actually occurred in 2007. The trial Judge was also concerned that the rates related to different vehicles and that given that the Claimant was only 23 it was not clear that ordinary hire companies would hire any vehicle, let alone a powerful vehicle, to him. As a result, at first instance the credit hire rates were awarded in full.

The Court of Appeal disagreed. In relation to the timing point, Jacob LJ giving the leading judgment held that:

> *"Working with comparables and making adjustments is the daily diet of judges concerned with valuation in all sorts of fields. <u>Clearly evidence of the spot rate a year or so later than the relevant date is likely to throw considerable light on what the spot rate would have been at the time.</u>"[14]*

In relation to whether the Defendant needed to provide rates evidence for an identical vehicle, Jacob LJ continued that:

> *"one must not be hypnotised by any supposed need to find an exact spot rate for an almost exactly comparable car. Normally, the replacement need be no more than in the same broad range of quality and nature as the damaged car. There may be a bracket of spot rates for cars rather "better" and rather "worse". A Judge who considered that bracket and aimed for some sort of reasonable average would not be going wrong."[15]*

Perhaps the unusual features of this decision will be immediately apparent. It certainly has the merit of brevity. The Court of Appeal judgment is barely more than two pages long. It makes very little reference to earlier jurisprudence and no reference at all to *Burdis v Livsey*. This might be thought surprising given that the suggestion that Judges could adopt "some sort of reasonable average" apparently contradicts the express rejection of averages in *Burdis*.

The result was that the issue of spot hire rates was then referred back to the County Court for determination at a fresh hearing at which the

---

14 *Bent no1* para 8.

15 *Bent no1*. para 9.

Claimant was allowed the opportunity to enter his own rates evidence. This sets the scene for the second Bent case in which the resulting assessment of the equivalent spot hire rate was appealed again, this time by the Claimant.

c) Bent no2

In order to explain this decision, it is necessary to start by setting out the facts in more detail. The Claimant, Darren Bent, was a well-known Premier League footballer. He was not impecunious. He was 23 at the time of the accident. He hired an Aston Martin DB9 as a replacement for his Mercedes-Benz CLS 63 AMG Coupe. It is perhaps unfortunate that a leading case on the calculation of spot hire rates should concern two such specialised and prestigious vehicles, when the vast majority of cases before the courts concern rather more standard vehicles.

The Claimant relied on written and oral evidence from the Chief Executive of the credit hire company, which attached tables of spot rates for vehicles in category SP9 in Spring 2009 and also further evidence about 2007 figures from smaller specialist hirers. The Defendant relied on a rates survey carried out on the internet and by telephone to gain the hire rates from five ordinary car hire companies.

The Court of Appeal began by setting out the legal background. As set out above, it confirmed that *"the damages recoverable for loss of use of the damaged car will be that sum which is attributable to the basic hire rate of the replacement car."*[16]

Thus far in this chapter, we have adopted the phrase 'spot hire rate' to reflect the market cost of hiring a replacement vehicle. This was the phrase used by Lord Hoffmann. However *Bent no2* states that "Spot hire rates" is a misnomer and that "it would be better if, in the context of credit hire cases, the term "spot rate" were not used in future and the term "basic hire rate" or BHR were used instead".[17] We will follow the

---

16 *Bent No2* para. 33.

17 *Ibid.* para. 34.

Court of Appeal's guidance and refer to basic hire rates from this point forwards.

The Court of Appeal continued that "*it is for a defendant to demonstrate, by evidence, that there is a difference between the credit hire charge agreed between the claimant and the credit hire company and the BHR*".[18] The Court of Appeal supported this proposition in a footnote by saying that it is well established that it is for the Defendant to prove that the Claimant has benefitted from betterment so that the damages recovered must be reduced.

The Court then considered how the basic hire rate might be established. It held that a court could consider two types of evidence: direct evidence and indirect evidence. Direct evidence would consist of "*published rates, from the actual credit hire company that hired the replacement car which demonstrates either that the credit hire rate and the BHR for that type of car is the same or it is different and what the difference is*". According to the Court, "*if there is such direct evidence it might be the best evidence of any difference between the credit hire rate charged and the BHR for that type of car in that area at the time the replacement car was hired*".[19] The second type of evidence, termed "indirect evidence", is "*evidence of the BHR charged by other car hire companies in the area for the type of car actually hired*".[20]

The reference to direct evidence might encourage credit hire companies to consider whether it would be in their interests to publish a basic hire rate tariff. They might argue that a credible tariff is all that is required to demonstrate the BHR, after all the Court of Appeal recognised that this might represent the "best evidence" on the point. Insurers might respond that this would be misleading because many credit hire organisations purely specialise in credit hire. Their rates are not available to

---

18 *Ibid.* para. 35 and note that the Court of Appeal repeated this at paragraph 73: "has the defendant proved a difference between the credit hire rate actually paid for the car hired and what, in the same broad geographical area, would have been the BHR for the model of car actually hired".

19 *Ibid.* para. 38.

20 *Ibid.* para. 41.

ordinary customers, or not attractive to them. Practical issues would likely arise in relation to the extent of disclosure which is proportionate and necessary to support any such tariff.

In returning to the case at hand, in a section headed discussion and conclusion, the Court restated the test: *"the aim of the judge's fact finding exercise is to ascertain the BHR for the model of car that the claimant actually hired and to do so on an objective basis".*[21] This was later confirmed by saying that on the facts the question was *"what was the BHR for the Aston Martin DB9 that was actually hired".*[22]

In considering the discussion of rates in *Burdis v Livsey*, the Court interpreted the earlier decision as meaning that *"the court has to calculate the BHR on the basis that the claimant notionally went round to an equivalent non-credit hire company. If there is a difference between the two rates [ie between credit hire and BHR], the claimant will recover the BHR that the non-credit car hire company would have charged, even if the BHR that the car hire company charged was at the top end of the range, provided that the claimant acted reasonably."*[23]

The logic of this passage may well be sound. But it rather avoids tackling the interesting question, which is whether the Court of Appeal i n *Burdis* was correct to place an initial evidential burden on the claimant.

In relation to the discussion of averages in *Bent no1*, the Court said that:

> *"it may be difficult to produce evidence of an exact BHR for the car that was actually hired on credit terms. The judge has to deal with the evidence available. It is in that sense that Jacob LJ said that a judge would not be going wrong if he considered a bracket of BHRs for cars rather better or rather worse than the one actually hired. But, whether the judge has evidence of BHRs for the type of car*

21 *Ibid.* para. 74.

22 *Ibid.* para. 80.

23 *Ibid.* para. 76.

actually hired on credit, or has evidence of BHRs for other types of car which are within a bracket that is comparable, the aim of the exercise remains the same. It is to make a calculation of what the BHR was for the car actually hired and so compare it with the credit hire rate actually paid.

"I do not believe that Jacob LJ intended to suggest that "some sort of reasonable average" of a bracket of "spot rates" for cars rather better or worse than that actually hired on credit terms would produce the BHR to which a claimant was entitled. Such an approach would be inconsistent with this Court's statement in Burdis v Livsey at [146], where it expressly rejected the suggestion that a claimant should recover the average cost of car hire, whether the actual cost to him was more or less than the average. I think that all Jacob LJ was doing was to give an indication of one way by which a judge might identify the BHR of the actual car hire on credit hire terms by mean of what, in [38] above, I have called indirect evidence"[24]

One possible confusion is that when turning back to paragraph 38, the reference there to indirect evidence is only to say that *"it is unlikely that indirect evidence from the car hire company (such as its assertion of what its BHR would have been had they had one) will be useful"*. This is plainly not the same indirect evidence referred to in the paragraph above. Perhaps the reference is misplaced and it should refer to paragraph 41 (evidence of hire rates charged by other companies) and not 38.

The reader might also be forgiven for emerging from these paragraphs wondering whether the use of averages is sanctioned or not. After all the judgment starts by noting that the Court of Appeal had expressly rejected the use of averages in *Burdis*, but appears to end by saying that what Jacobs LJ had suggested in *Bent No1* (which was the use of averages) was *"one way by which a judge might identify the BHR"*. Though *Bent No1* was plainly not followed, nor was it expressly said to be wrongly decided. Perhaps the point is simply that the Court of Appeal wished to make it clear that, where no rate is available for an

---

24 *Ibid.* paras 78 and 79.

exactly comparable vehicle, the Courts can still consider a bracket of rates for better and worse vehicles in arriving at a basic hire rate.

On the facts, the Court of Appeal concluded that the trial Judge had *"erred in concentrating on the 2009 figure when 2007 figures were available"*. Moreover *"the judge erred in concentrating on the range of figures for a Mercedes SL 55 AMG when BHR figures for an Aston Martin DB9 were available"*. The Court held that *"the best evidence on which to make a finding relates to the contemporaneous 2007 rates for an Aston Martin DB9."* These figures were available within the Claimant's rates evidence.

In relation to the Defendant's survey, whilst the Court described it as *"useful evidence"*, there was a flaw: *"all the quotations stipulated a minimum age for a driver, the lowest of which was 25…Mr Bent was, of course, 23 at the time"*. As a result, the claimant would have had to arrange cover through his own insurance, yet *"there is no firm evidence that Mr Bent's insurers would have been prepared to insure him to hire an Aston Martin DB9 so that it cannot be demonstrated that the lower rates discovered by Miss Goeting would have been applicable".*[25]

The result on the facts was that the Defence had failed to prove that that the BHR was lower than the credit hire rate and the Claimant therefore recovered the credit hire rate in full. This result cannot logically be limited to cases where there is a difficulty in hiring a vehicle based on the Claimant's age; Claimants may rely on this principle in all circumstances where the ordinary car hire companies will not hire to the Claimant, for instance where they have speeding convictions.

d) Stevens v Equity Syndicate Management

The fourth case to reach the Court of Appeal was *Stevens*. The Claimant had hired a replacement Audi A4 for a period of 28 days whilst his own vehicle was unroadworthy. An issue arose as to the recoverable rate of hire. At first instance, guided presumably by *Bent No1*, the Recorder

---

25 *Ibid.* paras 87 and 89.

allowed an average of four equivalent basic hire rates. It was agreed on appeal that adopting averages was not the correct approach.[26]

The Court of Appeal began by citing paragraph 73 of Bent No2 with approval, because it explains a structured approach which may usefully be adopted in these cases. Paragraph 73 of Bent No2 reads:-

> "to summarise, the questions are: (i) did the claimant need to hire a replacement car at all; if so, (ii) was it reasonable, in all the circumstances, to hire the particular type of car actually hired at the rate agreed; if it was (iii) was the claimant 'impecunious'; if not, (iv) has the defendant proved a difference between the credit hire rate actually paid for the car hired and what, in the same broad geographic area, would have been the BHR for the model of car actually hired and if so what is it; if so, (v) what is the difference between the credit hire rate and the BHR"

In the High Court, Burnett J had held that the search for the BHR should be for the figure that the claimant would have been willing to pay had he gone into the ordinary car hire market. That clearly indicated a subjective test based on what that specific Claimant would have done. Burnett J acknowledged this by indicating that "questioning of the claimant on this issue, should be directed to exploring what he would have been willing to pay on the hypothesis that he would have gone into the market to hire a vehicle".

The Court of Appeal rejected the subjective approach. It held that the reason for looking at basic hire rates is in order to strip out additional benefits from the credit hire contract. This is an objective exercise. Evidence about what the specific claimant would have done is "likely to be of very little assistance".[27]

The Court acknowledged that Courts "are still experiencing practical difficulties in calculating the BHR". It identified the problem as being

---

26 *Stevens* para. 25.

27 *Stevens* para. 39.

that the claims are often for small sums and lawyers and judges have to approach them "at proportionate cost".[28]

The Court also expressly acknowledged that some uncertainty is inherent in the nature of the exercise of assessing the BHR: *"any attempt to value the benefits at a later stage in a proportionate way must necessarily involve a degree of imprecision. The best that can be hoped for, absent a very expensive exercise of disclosure and analysis, is a reasonable approximation".*[29]

That goes some way to answering many of the criticisms that Claimants typically make of rates evidence. It suggests that exactly comparable rates are not required and a degree of imprecision is acceptable. The aim is to arrive at a practical and proportionate solution.

With proportionality in mind, the Court of Appeal concluded that: "the lowest reasonable rate quoted by a mainstream supplier for the hire of a vehicle to a person such as the claimant is a reasonable approximation to the BHR."[30] In so doing, it expressly rejected the Claimant's contention that he should recover the highest figure in the range of rates as "manifestly unjust" because it was the credit hire company that was in the best position to disclose its actual charging structure.[31]

A key passage sets out the principle:-

> *"it follows that a judge faced with a range of hire rates should try to identify the rate or rates for the hire, in the claimant's geographical area, of the type of car actually hired by the claimant on credit hire terms. If that exercise yields a single rate then that rate is likely to be a reasonable approximation for the BHR. If, on the other hand, it yields a range of rates then a reasonable estimate of the BHR may be obtained by identifying the lowest reasonable rate quoted by a*

---

28 *Ibid.* para. 30.

29 *Ibid.* para. 34.

30 *Ibid.* para. 35.

31 *Ibid.* para. 36.

mainstream supplier or, if there is no mainstream supplier, by a local reputable supplier."

Thus, it was for the defendant to prove that there was a difference between the BHR and the credit hire rate. If the defendant identifies a single basic hire rate, that is likely to be the measure of loss. If the defendant identifies a range of rates, the Court should adopt the lowest reasonable rate from a mainstream supplier. If there is no mainstream supplier, the Court should adopt the lowest reasonable rate from a local reputable supplier.

One final curiosity of the case is that the subjective rate adopted by Burnett J and the lowest reasonable rate adopted by the Court of Appeal both led to a figure only slightly less than the average which the Recorder had awarded (wrongly) at first instance.

e) Conclusion

It is difficult to offer the reader any certain conclusions, in circumstances where the thorny nature of the issue is demonstrated by the fact that it has gone before the Court of Appeal four times in the last 20 years. Despite the clear guidance in *Stevens*, hire rates still provide fertile ground for argument in the County Courts. As a result, we doubt that *Stevens* will really be the final word on this issue.

Standing back from the detail for a moment, the difficulty in these cases is usually that the Court is confronted by a range of different rates, sometimes provided by both parties and sometimes provided by the Defendant and rebutted by the Claimant, which can cover a range of different vehicles, terms and conditions and dates. But in order to award damages, the Court needs to arrive at a single figure. How should it turn the range of rates evidenced by the parties into a single basic hire rate?

It will not have escaped the reader's attention that each of the four Court of Appeal decisions advocates a different solution to this problem. Indeed, the whole spectrum of possible solutions has been advocated: in *Burdis* it appeared that the Court was suggesting that a figure towards the top of the range of rates should be selected, in *Bent no1* an average of the rates was put forward and, finally, in *Stevens* the lowest reasonable rate was selected. Despite these obvious contradictions, the more recent Court of Appeal decisions fail properly to explain why they depart from the previous decision. Perhaps this is because strictly speaking as a matter of precedent, the Court of Appeal cannot overrule itself – so at each stage, the Court must maintain that its new decision is consistent with previous authority. This is not helpful to the lawyer seeking a clear answer to the question - the section of *Bent no2* which attempts to reconcile its decision with *Bent no1* is particularly unconvincing.

The starting point in arguing rates evidence in practice must now be the decision in *Stevens*. It is the most recent decision. It is also the most straightforward to apply in practice – for Courts looking to find a single rate, it is easier to look for the lowest reasonable rate than to struggle with the more circuitous reasoning in *Bent No2*.

It is submitted that it is now clear that the burden of proof is on the Defendant to establish the BHR. Despite the ambiguous wording in *Burdis v Livsey*, *Bent no2* clearly places the burden of proof on the Defendant and *Stevens* agrees with *Bent no2* on that issue. Moreover, as explained in those cases, that result is also consistent with the law of betterment generally.

It is then clear that the task facing the court is to try to identify the BHR for the type of vehicle that the Claimant actually hired. In assessing this rate, in the absence of direct evidence of a basic hire tariff from the credit hire company, the best evidence would be evidence of the right type of vehicle in the right location and at the right time. However, Defendants may argue that the references in *Stevens* to a "reasonable approximation" and "a degree of imprecision" when read together with the statement in *Bent No1* – never expressly overruled – that one should not be "hypnotised" by a need to find an exactly comparable vehicle, suggest that the Courts need not reject rates evidence altogether if it does not exactly replicate the original hire.

Finally, although the guidance in *Stevens* that the Courts should adopt the "lowest reasonable rate" appears clear, a number of aspects of the decision leave arguments open to both parties. First, what exactly is meant by the lowest _reasonable_ rate? Claimants may argue that the word "reasonable" qualifies the rates that the Court should adopt so that the Court can discard any rates that impose onerous conditions such as a high deposit or excess. Defendants may argue that it only excludes rates which are obviously not comparable. Second, which hire companies qualify as "mainstream suppliers" or "local reputable suppliers"? Presumably, mainstream suppliers include household names such as Enterprise, Europcar or Avis. But what are the "mainstream" suppliers for more prestigious vehicles or private hire vehicles? And it is more difficult to identify what qualifies as a local reputable supplier. Where the hire companies involved are less well known, the Defendant may be well advised to ensure that the rates evidence addresses whether they are reputable suppliers though what exactly is required to meet this test remains open to argument. It is suggested that the number of years that a company has been established may well be relevant. But at one extreme, the parties could adduce evidence about online reviews of the company in an attempt to demonstrate that it is or is not reputable.

D. EVIDENTIAL MATTERS

Where the court is evaluating two pieces of rates evidence, in addition to considering which comes closest to demonstrating the BHR for the type of car actually hired, it will still have to weigh the credibility and reliability of the evidence in reaching its conclusions as to the BHR.

Advocates and lawyers working in this area will quickly develop their own approach to tackling the merits of different pieces of evidence. A 'menu' of the more common issues is set out below. But this is an area in which the devil always lies in the detail. Often this requires an analysis of the raw data, which is buried in annexes to a statement, to ensure that it really supports the summary table which is usually offered. Many of the best points need to be discovered on a case by case basis in the detail of individual items of evidence.

It is not our intention to comment on the litigation involving contempt of court allegations against the employees of a certain rates surveying company.[32] Suffice it to say that, returning to first principles, rates evidence is ordinary factual evidence and, like any other witness, the person who completed the survey must sign a statement of truth. The consequences if the statement of truth is compromised – including contempt of court - should in principle be no different for a witness as to basic hire rates than for any other witness.

Excess Waivers

In addition to the headline daily rate of hire, credit hire agreements often include additional daily charges in order to waive the excess applicable in the event that the car is damaged. These often reduce the applicable excess to zero. Claimants may scrutinise the Defendant's rates evidence to see whether the basic hire rates make an equivalent provision to waive all or some of the excess. Where they do not, it is open to the Claimant to argue that the Defendant's rates evidence should be rejected because it does not offer a true equivalent to the credit hire rate. Alternatively, Claimants may argue that the excess waiver charges should be added to the basic hire rate.

This remains an open issue. The Court of Appeal has never had to grapple directly with a case in which the issue of excess waivers had a potentially decisive impact on the rates evidence. In *Stevens*, although the Court of Appeal (and indeed Burnett J in the High Court) indicated that the Recorder "properly focussed" on rates "with a nil excess"[33] that was in the context of a case in which some of the Defendant's rates did had a nil excess and the issue does not appear to have been argued in any detail.

Claimants may argue that they are entitled to hire with a nil excess. The authorities provide some support for these submissions, at least to the

---

32 For a summary of the facts, see *Dickinson and others v Tesco Plc and others* [2013] EWCA Civ 36.

33 *Stevens* para. 40.

extent that they suggest that it is reasonable for a replacement vehicle to be provided with a nil excess. Thus in *Marcic v Davies*[34], the Defendant sought to argue that collision damage waiver incorporated an element of betterment because the Claimant's own policy did not have a nil excess. Browne-Wilkinson LJ held that:-

> *"I do not accept that submission. In accordance with the ordinary rule of damages the plaintiff is entitled to be put back, as far as possible, into the position in which he would have been had the collision not occurred. If there had been no collision the plaintiff would never have come under any contractual liability to the car hire company. It was accepted that it was reasonable for him to hire the car from the car hire company. Since he could only do this by effecting comprehensive insurance in the full amount or by bearing the excess of £150, if he had elected to bear the excess himself, he would, under the terms of his hiring contract with the hire company, have come under a contractual liability to pay £150 to the hire company in respect of damage. What is more, that would be damage not to his own motor car but to hire company's motor car. Accordingly, this liability for £150 that he would have had to the hire company if he had not paid the waiver fee would have been a contractual obligation which he would never have been under had it not been for the original collision with the defendant...*
>
> *The element of betterment to which Mr Tudor Evans referred would only have arisen if during the period of the hire the plaintiff had in fact had a further accident. It is true that if that had happened to his own motor car he would have had to bear the whole cost of the damage to his motor car if he had decided to have it repaired, whereas if the hired car had crashed during that period he would not have had to bear such cost. But in fact no such accident occurred. What we are concerned with is the cost of covering the plaintiff against a contractual liability that he was bound to enter into and the cost of so doing. In my judgment the learned*

---

34 Court of Appeal, 20 February 1985.

judge was right to include the waiver fee as an item of recoverable damage."

The point was revisited in *Bee v Jenson*[35] before Morison J. He commented that "had the point been live, I would have held that it was reasonable for the replacement vehicle to have been provided with a nil excess regardless of the excess that applied to Mr Bee's own car." His reasoning was that rather than being a betterment, the collision damage waiver is a reasonable arrangement consequential on the tort.

Morison J also referred to *Marcic v Davies*. He accepted that the case was binding on him and added "I have no hesitation in following it". Nevertheless, as the first quotation above indicates, this point was not live in *Bee v Jenson* and Morison J's comments are *obiter*.

Defendants may argue that whilst these authorities confirm that a nil excess may be reasonable in principle, this does not give hire companies a licence to charge whatever they choose to provide the nil excess. There must come a point where the amount charged for excess waivers becomes so high that it is itself unreasonable.

Defendants may also seek to address this issue through their own rates evidence. The ideal evidence for the Defendant would, of course, be a basic hire rate which includes a charge to limit the excess to the same level as the credit hire rate. Often this is not possible, either because this information goes beyond what is readily available on an internet quotation, or simply because the basic hire company cannot match the credit hire companies' waiver. In this case, Defendants may have to rely on evidence of the cost to obtain an excess waiver from a third party.

This last option is controversial. A number of specialist providers can offer quotations online to reduce or eliminate an insurance excess. Defendants may argue that this offers a complete solution to the excess waiver. Claimants may argue that, first, the Claimant was not aware that such insurance was available. This obviously depends on the facts, and to some extent on the level of involvement of the Claimant's

---

35 [2006] EWHC 3359.

insurer / broker. Second, the Claimant may argue that it is simply not reasonable to expect the victim of a road traffic accident to go to the trouble of sourcing a car from one company and an excess waiver from another. Third, the Claimant may wish to check the full terms and conditions of the waiver provider to see whether they really do match the credit hire waiver.

In the absence of express guidance from the higher courts, it is not surprising that different results have been reached in the County Court in relation to these issues. In *Dhami v Amlin Corporate Member Ltd*,[36] the Court found in the Claimant's favour that a basic hire rate with an applicable excess of £3,000 was not genuinely equivalent to the credit hire rate with a nil excess. In so doing, the Court rejected the third party insurance provider because there was no evidence that an online excess waiver was a product that could reasonably be found by the claimant. The same result was reached after *Stevens* in *Cheung v UK Insurance Ltd*.[37]

Other cases have taken a different approach. In *Lawson v Mullen*,[38] the Court concluded that the Claimant does not have an "inalienable right" to a nil excess. Rather the overarching question is one of reasonableness. On the facts of that case, where the credit hire rate was around £150 per day more expensive than a basic hire rate with a £500 excess, it was unreasonable not to select the basic hire rate.

There must be some force in the conclusion in *Lawson* that there is no inalienable right to a nil excess. Otherwise, to take an extreme case, the Claimant could recover excess waiver charges which are higher than the excess itself. If it is correct that the real question is one of reasonableness, then much will depend on the facts of the case. It might be observed that the obvious difference between the facts of *Lawson* and the facts of *Dhami* and *Cheung* was the size of the excess applicable to the basic hire rate. Where the excess applicable to the basic hire rate runs into thousands of pounds, it is likely to be more difficult to per-

---

36 Unreported, HHJ Oliver Jones QC, 23 July 2013.

37 Unreported, HHJ Worster, 27 March 2015.

38 Unreported, HHJ Freedman, 12 June 2015.

suade a Court that a claimant ought reasonably to have taken that option. Conversely, where the excess applicable is more limited, it becomes more difficult for the Claimant to argue that it was reasonable to take the credit hire rate in order to avoid the excess.

Methodology

It is sometimes worth attacking the methodology of the rates survey. The aim is to demonstrate either that it is not truly representative of the basic hire market or that the resulting rates would not really have been available to the claimant. The following points can arise:-

a) the rates may not be comparable with the rate offered by the credit hire company. In addition to the excess waivers addressed above, the basic hire rates might impose a mileage restriction or limit the number of additional drivers;

b) where the hire lasts for more than 28 days or even more than 7 days, the BHR may be based on a discount for the number of days hired. Depending on the evidence, the Claimant might argue that he did not know at the start of the hire period how long he needed the hire vehicle for. This might have the result that the claimant would have been unable to take advantage of the discounted rate.

In *Bent no2*, the Court of Appeal rejected the submission that the trial Judge was wrong to take the 28 day rate. At paragraph 90, the reason given was that it was clear from the outset that *"it was going to take a considerable time to effect the repairs on this specialist car which needed specialist parts that had to come from Germany."*

It is worth noting two features of this decision. First, claimants may argue that it follows from that decision that it might be appropriate to take a daily or a 7 day rate in any case where it would <u>not</u> have been clear to the claimant that repairs were going to take a long time.

Second, the result reached in *Bent no2* is puzzling. At paragraph 91, the Court of Appeal accepted the trial Judge's finding that there was a discount to the daily rate in respect of longer hires and therefore discounted the BHR by 12%. It is not clear where this figure of 12% came from (the suggestion is that it was a concession by counsel at first instance, though what the concession was based on remains unclear). But in the absence of any statistics to support it, is this not an arbitrary discount of the type criticized by the Court of Appeal in *Burdis v Livsey*?

c) the person obtaining the rates evidence is likely to be a specialist in carrying out similar surveys. They may therefore be in a better position than the Claimant would have found himself in. In this regard, it is particularly important to consider how the witness selected which companies to ask for a quote. Have they selected companies that they know belong at either the top or bottom end of the market? Have they only been able to source a vehicle after a series of referrals?

d) It is worth checking whether the basic hire rates come from a genuinely local company, or local branch of a national company, rather than from a London company which offers a delivery service;

e) If the Claimant uses their vehicle for business use, it is necessary to check whether the basic hire rates allow for business use;

f) Beware in particular of rates from hire companies located at airports. These companies are likely to be targeting the specific tourist market, they may well be in direct competition with a number of other companies in close proximity. They may not be truly representative of the local market as a result;

g) Where the rates evidence covers a selection of vehicles, it is worth considering whether these vehicles are truly comparable to the vehicle actually hired. A common flaw in rates evidence is that it assumes a certain level of knowledge about models of car, and neglects to explain properly why they are considered to be comparable;

h) In line with the decision in *Stevens*, it is now permissible to investigate whether the hire companies involved are "mainstream" and whether they are "reputable local suppliers".

In many lower value claims it is common for rates evidence to be assessed on paper only. It is usually to the advantage of the person seeking to challenge the rates evidence to try to get the witness to attend court for cross-examination. Unexpected flaws may become apparent under questioning.

Credibility

Another way to attack rates evidence, in appropriate cases, is to undermine the credibility of the witness who puts the rates forward. Often their objectivity might be challenged, particularly if the witness is linked to the credit hire company or to the insurer. Alternatively, it might be worth exploring what proportion of their instructions come from claimants and defendants (as a litigant would assess a medical expert in a personal injury case) and how much they get paid for each statement.

A related point is that some cases suggest that witness statements (therefore including evidence of hire rates) should not be given by a solicitor with conduct of the case. This point was taken in a credit hire context in *TNT UK Ltd v Gregory*, in which the Court described the rule that a solicitor should not give evidence as "well-established" and explained that it was necessary to prevent conflicts of interest.[39]

---

39 TNT UK Ltd v Gregory and Choudry, Unreported, HHJ Hampton, 25 June 2010 para. 9.

The Form of Rates Evidence

A dispute sometimes arises about whether rates evidence is expert evidence. Procedurally, permission is required to rely on an expert report. Evidentially, the crucial difference is that an expert witness may give opinion evidence. Defendants may seek permission to rely on expert evidence on rates, in order to lend extra authority to their evidence or to allow their witness to answer questions with their opinion. By contrast, particularly on the small claims track where the courts are reluctant to give permission for expert evidence, the Claimant may argue that the rates evidence is expert and should be excluded. Defendants may respond by arguing that a person who carries out a survey is not exercising any particular expertise. Simply contacting hire companies is a task that anyone could perform. The point is arguable either way, however, many Courts now adopt a standard direction in relation to rates evidence, which specifies that it is factual evidence to be given in the form of a witness statement.

Where a witness is giving lay evidence about basic hire rates, unless the directions specify otherwise, the usual rules of evidence apply. This means that if the party does not intend to call the witness to give oral evidence, they must give the other party notice of this intention (different rules and considerations apply on the small claims track). Failure to do so could have serious consequences, including the exclusion of the evidence. *hearsay notices*

In small claims, where the strict rules of evidence do not apply, Defendants might choose to rely simply on quotations printed from the internet, perhaps even without a witness statement in support. In support of this approach, Defendants may rely on *Smith v Burney*.[40] In that case HHJ Behrens QC upheld the decision at first instance to admit evidence of basic hire rates which was simply printed off the internet and was sent to the Claimant's Solicitors only three working days before trial. The Court held that there was no prejudice to the Claimant since the evidence was easily verifiable and the limitations of the evidence were apparent on its face without the need for cross-exam-

---

40 Unreported, HHJ Behrens QC, 27 April 2007.

ination. Insurers may rely on this case to support the admission of evidence printed off the internet, and indeed late evidence of basic hire rates mores generally. Claimants may argue that the decision was influenced by the fact that this was an extremely small claim, worth less than £1,000. The same approach might not apply even to cases still within the small claims track but worth say £9,500.

Simultaneous Exchange or Rebuttal Evidence

The usual rule in civil cases is that the parties exchange their evidence at the same time, so that neither party has the benefit of seeing the other's evidence first. However, in a number of recent cases, the Claimant has argued that rather than filing their own rates evidence simultaneously, the Claimant should be permitted to file evidence rebutting the Defendant's rates. County Court practice is currently inconsistent. The Claimant's argument was accepted by District Judge Bloom in *Gonzalez v Dignity Funerals Ltd*[41] but rejected by District Judge Bell in *Miller v AIG Europe Ltd*.[42]

ABI Rates

It is not appropriate for Defendants to rely upon ABI Rates. As the Court of Appeal said in *Burdis* at paragraph 150:

> *"No doubt the scheme is, and will be, of benefit to insurers, the accident hire companies and the public; but the ABI figures cannot be taken in hostile litigation as being the appropriate figures of loss. They reflect a compromise agreed between the parties rather than an assessment of loss."*

The simple truth is that the ABI Rates are not relevant to the court's task in these cases. They will be left out of account.

---

41 Unreported, Willesden County Court, 14 March 2016.

42 Unreported, Guildford County Court, 15 January 2016.

CHAPTER TWO
IMPECUNIOSITY

A. Introduction
B. Lagden v O'Connor
C. Cases Applying Impecuniosity
D. Practical Issues

A. INTRODUCTION

There is only one clearly recognised exception to the rule in Di*mond v Lovell*. It arises where the Claimant was impecunious at the time of the hire. As we will see, the precise definition of impecuniosity remains contentious, but the essence of impecuniosity is that, at the relevant time, the Claimant could not afford to pay the basic hire rate.

In this chapter, we will consider the analysis of impecuniosity in the leading case of *Lagden v O'Connor*[1], with particular emphasis on the definition of impecuniosity and the practical implications of this issue.

B. LAGDEN v O'CONNOR

The Facts of Lagden

At first instance, HHJ Harris found as facts that Mr Lagden was:-

> "*an unusual man, an ex press photographer, now an unemployed Jehovah's witness in poor physical and mental health, with memory difficulties and a house on Canvey Island. He had very little money, he was indeed at all material times subject to an administration order.*"[2]

From these facts HHJ Harris drew the conclusion that Mr Lagden had no other choice but to enter a credit hire contract.[3]

---

1   *Lagden v O'Connor*, [2004] 1 AC 1067.
2   *Lagden*, para. 34.
3   *Ibid*, para. 82.

These findings are intriguing. The factual findings about Mr Lagden's means are remarkably brief. The Judgment gives no detail at all about whether Mr Lagden had any available savings, nor does it stop to analyse his income and outgoings. There is nothing in the Judgment to suggest that detailed disclosure was obtained or considered.

As a result, there is room to doubt the factual basis for the legal conclusion that he was impecunious. Lord Scott, in the minority of the House of Lords, drew attention to this: *"I do not regard the factual basis on which Dimond v Lovell has been distinguished as very persuasive...the proposition that Mr Lagden had no choice does not seem to me satisfactorily based given the rather sparse facts."*[4]

Moreover, these findings were made against a background of doubts about the claimant's credibility. HHJ Harris held that *"Mr Lagden was not a wholly convincing witness...he seemed for no very obvious reason to be anxious to assist Helphire if he could"*.[5] It is interesting that the courts were content to make a finding of impecuniosity against this limited factual background. Perhaps the explanation is that, given the administration order, Mr Lagden's case was so clear-cut that no further detail was required. As set out below, in most cases a more comprehensive analysis of the claimant's means is likely to be required.

The Principle Established in Lagden

In *Lagden*, the Claimant argued that it is one thing to say that credit hire rates incorporate irrecoverable additional benefits and so an ordinary claimant can only recover the equivalent basic hire rate. But it is quite another to apply this principle without modification to an impecunious claimant. Such a claimant could not afford to pay hire charges and so does not have a choice between the credit hire rate and the basic hire rate: for him / her it is credit hire or nothing. The argument runs that for such a person the additional benefits inherent in a credit hire contract are incidental to the cost of obtaining a

---

4   *Ibid,* paras 74-75.

5   *Ibid,* para. 35.

replacement vehicle. Therefore, the Claimant argued, an impecunious claimant should recover the credit hire charges in full.

The Insurers responded that this line of argument was foreclosed by the House of Lords decision in *Dimond* itself, which established a clear principle which did not allow for any exceptions. Moreover they relied on *the Liesbosch*[6] to assert that where damages are augmented by the Claimant's lack of financial resources, those additional damages are too remote to be recoverable from the Defendant.

By a narrow majority, the House of Lords found in favour of the Claimant.

Lord Hope delivered the most detailed of the three speeches in the majority. He began by setting out the House of Lords decision in *Dimond*. Then he described the problem in the following terms:

> *"But what if the injured party has no choice? What if the only way that is open to him to minimise his loss is by expending money which results in an incidental and additional benefit which he did not seek but the value of which can nevertheless be identified? Does the law require gain to be balanced against loss in these circum-stances? If it does, he will be unable to recover all the money that he had to spend in mitigation. So he will be at risk of being worse off than he was before the accident. That would be contrary to the ele-mentary rule that the purpose of an award of damages is to place the injured party in the same position as he was before the accident as nearly as possible."*[7]

He reviewed the authorities and concluded:

> *"the facts in these two cases were quite different from those in this case. But I think that the principles on which they were decided are of general application, and it is possible to extract this guidance*

---

6   *Owners of Liesbosch Dredger v Owners of SS Edison* ("the Liesbosch"), [1933] AC 449.

7   *Lagden*, para. 30.

from them. It is for the defendant who seeks a deduction from expenditure in mitigation on the ground of betterment to make out his case for doing so. It is not enough that an element of betterment can be identified. It has to be shown that the claimant had a choice, and that he would have been able to mitigate his loss at less cost… So if the evidence shows that the claimant had a choice, and that the route to mitigation which he chose was more costly than an alternative which was open to him, then a case will have been made out for a deduction. But if it shows that the claimant had no other choice available to him, the betterment must be seen as incidental to the step which he was entitled to take in the mitigation of his loss and there will be no ground for it to be deducted" [8]

And he later repeated:

"But it is reasonably foreseeable that there will be some car owners who will be unable to produce an acceptable credit or debit card and will not have the money in hand to pay for the hire in cash before collection. In their case the cost of paying for the provision of additional services by a credit hire company must be attributed in law not to the choice of the motorist but to the act or omission of the wrongdoer. That is Mr Lagden's case. In law the money which he spent to obtain the services of the credit hire company is recoverable." [9]

One criticism of these passages in Lord Hope's speech is that they seem to elide issues arising from mitigation and issues arising from betterment. It is striking that Lord Hope often refers to both issues in one sentence, which creates the impression that the same conclusions necessarily apply to both. Of course this is not necessarily the case, as the House of Lords decision in *Dimond* itself demonstrated.

Lord Hope also rejected the Defendant's arguments based on *The Liesbosch*. In that case the House of Lords had held that the damages payable by a Defendant could not be increased by virtue of a Claimant's

---

8 *Ibid*, para. 34.

9 *Ibid*, para. 37.

impecuniosity. Lord Hope stopped short of saying that *the Liesbosch* was wrongly decided. However, he said that: *"it is clear that the law has moved on"*.[10] In the same paragraph he continued that, the present position is that a wrongdoer must take his victim as he finds him: *"this rule applies to the economic state of the victim in the same way as it applies to his physical and mental vulnerability"*.

The other two majority speeches were shorter. Lord Nicholls (with whom Lord Slynn agreed) attacked the case from a common sense point of view:

> *"the law would be seriously defective if in this type of case the innocent motorist were, in practice, unable to obtain the use of a replacement car. The law does not assess damages payable to an innocent plaintiff on the basis that he is expected to perform the impossible. The common law prides itself on being sensible and reasonable. It has regard to practical realities"*.[11]

In the same paragraph he continued

> *"Here, as elsewhere, a negligent driver must take his victim as he finds him. Common fairness requires that if an innocent plaintiff cannot afford to pay car hire charges, so that left to himself he would be unable to obtain a replacement car to meet the need created by the negligent driver, then the damages payable under this head of loss should include the reasonable costs of a credit hire company"*.

The result of *Lagden* is thus that a claimant who was impecunious at the time of hire can, subject to any arguments about mitigation, recover the credit hire daily rate.

---

10 *Ibid,* para. 61.

11 *Ibid,* para. 6.

The Definition of Impecuniosity

It is plain from the dissenting speeches that Lord Scott and Lord Walker were concerned that it would prove difficult to give a workable definition of impecuniosity. Thus Lord Scott said *"the impecuniosity, no other choice, exception that your Lordships are introducing…is conceptually imprecise. It will, I believe, prove an obstacle to the swift and economical settlement of a very large number of simple cases. I think it will be a disservice to the development of the law".*[12]

Lord Walker expressed himself in similar terms: *"The concept of a claimant being unable to hire a replacement car (otherwise than through an accident hire company) because of impecuniosity is, as was acknowledged in the course of argument, a vague one… To allow the exception would be liable to lead to an increase in contested small claims, contrary to the public interest."*[13]

It is easy to understand the minority's concern. The Courts (and, of course, the parties) need to resolve many low value credit hire cases in a proportionate and fair way. But questions related to a claimant's means are inevitably fact specific, may require significant volumes of disclosure and may be open to different interpretations. As a result, whether or not the claimant falls within the definition of impecuniosity is often a contentious issue.

Lord Nicholls and Lord Hope both discussed the definition of impecuniosity. We will consider the relevant passages in both speeches and whether there is any substantial difference in their approaches.

The first definition of impecuniosity was suggested by Lord Nicholls:

> *"There remains the difficult point of what is meant by 'impecunious' in the context of the present type of case. Lack of financial means is, almost always, a question of priorities. In the present context what it signifies is inability to pay car hire charges without*

---

12 *Ibid*, para. 88.
13 *Ibid*, para. 106.

making sacrifices the plaintiff could not reasonably be expected to make."[14]

Thus Lord Nicholls propounded one single test: was the claimant unable to pay car hire charges without making sacrifices that he / she could not reasonably be expected to make.

Lord Nicholls himself described this test as "open-ended", thereby showing that he appreciated that this might give rise to difficulties in applying it to the facts of real cases. Of course, there will be a number of claimants who are obviously impecunious (like Mr Lagden) and obviously pecunious (perhaps having significant savings). But a significant number of claimants will fall somewhere in the middle; they would be able to raise the money to pay for hire charges, but using the money for hire charges would have a knock on effect on the rest of their finances. Should the law treat these individuals as impecunious? The answer according to Lord Nicholls is that the court should look at the sacrifices that the claimant would have to make in order to pay the hire charges, and determine if they are reasonable or unreasonable. But the problem is that this incorporates ideas of reasonableness which can lead to uncertainty; the reasonableness of particular decisions is inherently open to argument on the facts of individual cases.

Applying Lord Nicholls' test, the courts must consider a wide range of circumstances. One claimant might have had the right sum of money saved in a bank account, but have intended the money to pay for a family holiday. Another claimant might have £20,000 in savings, but say that this was a redundancy payment which they needed to keep in case they weren't able to find a new job. To take a more extreme example, another claimant might have £200,000 in a savings account but give evidence that they intended to use the money immediately to buy a yacht which they needed to maintain their status as the yacht club president. It is open to argument whether the sacrifices required of any or all of these hypothetical claimants in order to pay for hire charges would be reasonable or unreasonable and hence whether they would be regarded as impecunious.

---

14 *Ibid*, para. 9 (underlining added).

A different definition of impecuniosity was set out in the speech of Lord Hope. He began by saying:

> *"The wrongdoer is not entitled to demand of the injured party that he incur a loss, bear a burden or make unreasonable sacrifices in the mitigation of his damages."*[15]

This, of course, sounds similar to the test suggested by Lord Nicholls: where one judge in the majority speaks of *"unreasonable sacrifices"* and another judge in the majority speaks of *"sacrifices the plaintiff could not reasonably be expected to make"*, it seems artificial to try to draw a distinction between them. There is, however, something odd about the wording chosen by Lord Hope because incurring hire charges will always mean incurring a loss and bearing a burden. In fact, it transpires from the following paragraphs that Lord Hope had a rather different test in mind. He continued in the very next sentence:-

> *"He [the defendant] is entitled to demand that, where there are choices to be made, the least expensive route which will achieve mitigation must be selected".*

In expanding on the meaning of impecuniosity, Lord Hope returned to the notion of choice:-

> *"the criterion that must be applied is whether he had a choice – whether it would have been open to him to go into the market and hire a car at the ordinary rates from an ordinary car hire company.*[16]

> *In practice, for reasons that are obvious, companies which offer cars for hire in the open market insist on payment of the rental up front before the car is collected, together with a sum to cover the risk of damage to the car while it is on hire. Payment is usually made by*

---

15 *Ibid*, para. 34.
16 *Ibid*, para. 34.

means of a credit card or a debit card. Some companies may accept cash, but if they do the sum that will have to be paid up front will not be small. Many car owners are, of course, well able to provide what is needed to satisfy the hirer that the money which is needed to pay for the hire is available. If they choose to use the services of a credit hire company they must accept as a deduction from their expenditure the extra cost of doing so. The full cost of obtaining the services of a credit hire company cannot be claimed by the motorist who is able to pay the cost of the hire up front without exposing himself or his family to a loss or burden which is unreasonable.

But it is reasonably foreseeable that there will be some car owners who will be unable to produce an acceptable credit or debit card and will not have the money in hand to pay for the hire in cash before collection. In their case the cost of paying for the provision of additional services by a credit hire company must be attributed in law not to the choice of the motorist but to the act or omission of the wrongdoer."[17]

It is submitted that these passages indicate that the test which Lord Hope propounds is a test of choice: whether or not it would be 'open to' the Claimant to pay basic hire charges.

Clearly this test would produce different results compared with the test suggested by Lord Nicholls. In the examples previously given, the yacht club president, the redundant worker and the person saving for a family holiday all have a choice – it would be 'open to' all of them to hire a vehicle. As a result, applying Lord Hope's test all would be pecunious. The advantage of the test described by Lord Hope is that it is clearcut and easy to apply. The disadvantage is that it does not allow the Court to take account of an individual claimant's needs and circumstances and, as a result, it is capable of leading to unattractive results in practice.

The minority did not agree that "choice" was a workable test. Lord Scott commented that *"there are nearly always choices"* and continued that *"to say that he [Mr Lagden] had no other choice seems to me somewhat*

17 *Ibid*, paras 35 – 37.

implausible".[18] Lord Walker agreed, suggesting that the test is rather artificial: *"the choice is likely to depend on temperament and resource-fulness, rather than on some minute calculation of their margin of solvency."*[19]

In an attempt to answer the criticism that the test for impecuniosity would lead to an increase in contested cases, Lord Hope laid down a rule of thumb:

> *"In practice the dividing line is likely to lie between those who have, and those who do not have, the benefit of a recognised credit or debit card. It ought to be possible to identify those cases where the selection has been made on grounds of convenience only without much difficulty."*[20]

Again, the advantage of this rule of thumb is that it would bring clarity and certainty. It is straightforward to establish whether any individual claimant had a debit / credit card.

But, claimants may argue that such a test is too blunt an instrument. Lord Scott pointed out two problems with it. First, he said that *"there are still many people in this country who keep cash in their houses, would be accounted quite well-off by most standards, but who do not have credit or debit cards."*[21] Whether or not this remains factually accurate, the basic point remains that possession of a credit or debit card is not a true guide to wealth. It is easy to imagine a claimant with many credit cards, all with varying amounts of debt on them, being in a far worse financial position than a person with no credit cards.

Second, Lord Scott pointed out that there will be many people who lack spare cash to pay for hire charges, but could make use of a facility to borrow – perhaps through a credit card. The result of Lord Hope's test is that Mr Lagden who had no spare cash and so made use of credit

---

18 *Ibid*, para. 75.
19 *Ibid*, para. 106.
20 *Ibid*, para. 42.
21 *Ibid*, para. 87.

hire could recover the cost of credit inherent in the hire charges. But another claimant who had no spare cash but could have paid for hire charges on a credit card, would logically only recover the basic hire rate and so could not recover the cost of credit. Lord Scott suggested that no sensible distinction can be drawn between these cases – they simply involve claimants using different sources of credit.

This in turn raises the spectre of whether a claimant who could only afford to pay for basic hire charges on a credit card can increase his damages by claiming the cost of the basic hire charges plus the cost to him of putting those basic hire charges on his credit card (i.e. the interest on those charges). Although inevitably difficult to calculate (it would depend on the terms applicable to his credit card), since the Liesbosch is no longer good law, claimants may argue that there is no barrier to such a claim.

As set out above, there are differences between the approach adopted by Lord Nicholls and Lord Hope. No subsequent higher court cases have expressed a preference for one test over the other. As a result, defendants may wish to emphasise Lord Hope's more clear-cut test of 'choice', whilst Claimants may prefer to emphasise Lord Nicholls' test of 'unreasonable sacrifices'. There remains ample scope for argument on the facts of specific cases.

Further issues of principle remain to be resolved. For example, how far is the court entitled to take account of the earnings of the Claimant's partner in determining impecuniosity? In this context, the case of *Fettes v Williams*[22] is interesting because HHJ Hull QC was quite prepared to take account of the Claimant's husband's earnings in deciding that she was not impecunious.

C. CASES APPLYING IMPECUNIOSITY

Although there are few reported appeals and it would not be practical to set out every first instance decision on impecuniosity, it may be helpful

---

22 Fettes v Williams, HHJ Hull QC, unreported 22 January 2003.

to set out a number of decisions below as an illustration of the way in which the courts apply the definitions of impecuniosity in real cases.

In the High Court in *Stevens v Equity Syndicate Management Ltd*,[23] the Claimant appealed a finding that he was not impecunious. Burnett J described the factual evidence as "sketchy": the Claimant's witness statement asserted briefly that he could not have afforded to pay for hire charges and statements had been adduced from one current bank account which showed a balance between £2,500 and £3,500 whilst his car was with the repairer.[24] He also had an overdraft facility of £1,000. Hire charges at the basic hire rate were assessed at less than £1,500.

However, the Claimant asserted that once he had paid his mortgage and a loan, he only had around £500 per month for all other expenses (in fact, the analysis of his accounts suggested that the surplus was £750 not £500 but nothing turns on this). In oral evidence he added that he needed to keep a cushion of money to protect him against future events and gave the example that he later had to find money to pay for a child to have a tonsillectomy.

Burnett J concluded that the trial Judge was entitled to find that the Claimant was not impecunious and to base that finding on the "continuous healthy balance" in his current account.[25]

There are two interesting features of the decision. First, Burnett J noted that the single bank account disclosed "could not conceivably reflect the totality of economic activity of a man, still less a family man". Few withdrawals were evident from the current account, including no cash withdrawals and only one related to a supermarket and one relating to petrol. The plain inference must either be that the claimant or his family had access to another account or he dealt largely in cash. This shows that it can be important for defendants to look beyond the basic

---

23 *Stevens v Equity Syndicate Management Ltd*, [2014] EWHC 689. As set out in Chapter One, the Claimant appealed to the Court of Appeal on the rates issue but not on the impecuniosity issue.

24 *Ibid*, para. 18.

25 *Ibid*, para. 21.

figures in bank accounts and to question whether they really reflect the claimant's full financial position.

Second, Burnett J remarked that the trial Judge was entitled to find that the claimant was not impecunious *"particularly in the context of a case where there was no dispute on liability and thus no question about the recoverability of reasonable hire charges"*.[26] This reasoning has not been explored in other cases. But it raises an interesting question. Should the Courts assess whether it was open to the claimant to pay hire charges / whether the claimant could pay hire charges without making unreasonable sacrifices in absolute terms or on the basis that the claimant would have to part with money upfront but then be reimbursed? Defendants may argue that *Stevens* suggests that it is more difficult for a claimant to establish that he/she could not afford to pay hire charges, where liability is not in dispute and hence the claimant could expect to be repaid the money within a relatively short period. Claimants may respond that the issue is really about what they could afford at a particular moment in time and how likely they are to be able to recover the money – which may not be obvious at the time - is unlikely to be determinative.

In *Thompson v Vincent Haulage Ltd,*[27] a claimant with savings of £2,000 and a credit limit on his credit card of £1,000 was found not to impecunious in circumstances where the evidence suggested a basic hire rate in the region of £2,400. The argument that the claimant intended to use the £2,000 for the purchase of a property in Bulgaria was rejected partly for lack of evidence and partly because there was no indication that the money was required "within a short time".[28]

In *Boardman v Byrne,*[29] the claimant's assertion that he was impecunious was rejected based partly on his own admission that he would probably have been able to borrow the money and partly due to the

---

26 *Ibid*, para. 21.

27 HHJ Benson QC, Preston County Court, 15 April 2008, unreported.

28 *Ibid*, para. 21.

29 Walsall County Court, 18 April 2008, unreported.

"enormous resources" of the claimant's business which was the part owner of the damaged vehicle.[30]

In *W v Veolia Environmental Services UK (PLC),*[31] the evidence suggested that the claimant actuary was only earning enough to cover the costs of his business. He had not taken a salary for five years. He was under financial pressure due to an earlier divorce and he was likely to retire in not many more years. He was overdrawn at the time, but had an overdraft facility of up to £30,000. He had savings of £50,000 - £100,000. He also had income from pensions, bringing in around £20,000 per annum.[32] The basic hire rate was in the region of £485 per day.[33] HHJ Mackie QC held that the Claimant was impecunious.[34] His credit cards would not have withstood the basic hire rate for more than a brief period. He reasonably needed his limited capital for his old age.

D. **PRACTICAL ISSUES**

Burden of Proof

One issue which has been controversial is which party bears the burden of proving whether or not the claimant was impecunious.

An issue arose as to the burden of proof in relation to whether the Claimant could have afforded to repair / replace his vehicle in the Court of Appeal decision in *Zurich Insurance Plc v Umerji.*[35] In that case as a result of the directions order, having failed to disclose all his financial documents, the claimant was debarred from relying on impecuniosity. The Court of Appeal held that that debarring order applied to all issues

---

30 *Ibid,* para. 15.2.

31 [2011] EWHC 2010.

32 All findings of fact in this regard are set out in paragraph 7 of the judgment.

33 The Claimant hired a new Bentley in replacement for his 21 year old Bentley, explaining the scale of the basic hire rate. Perhaps a different result might have been reached had the Defendant challenged the reasonableness of hiring a new Bentley as a replacement.

34 *Ibid,* para. 61.

35 [2014] EWCA Civ 357.

to which the Claimant's finances were relevant. It considered that it made no practical sense to treat the burden of proof regarding impecuniosity differently as regards mitigation or as regards rates – the concept is the same and depends on the same evidence.[36] It added that since a claim for hire charges is a claim for expenditure incurred in mitigation of the primary loss (the loss of use of a vehicle), the burden is on the claimant to "prove (and therefore plead) that such expenditure was reasonably incurred".[37] Whilst this discussion was primarily in relation to the burden of proof on mitigation and the meaning of a specific unless order, it is plain from the discussion that the Court of Appeal considered that the burden of proof in relation to impecuniosity (as it applies to rates) was on the Claimant.

Claimants may argue that this is not consistent with earlier authorities which suggested that it was for the Defendant to prove that the Claimant was not impecunious. Thus Lord Hope in *Lagden* had said that *"it is for the defendant who seeks a deduction from expenditure in mitigation on grounds of betterment to make out his case for doing so…it has to been shown that the claimant had a choice."*[38] That approach was supported by the cases on betterment cited in that case.

Defendants, however, may argue that the burden of proof properly rests on the Claimant for three reasons. First, it is the Claimant who asserts that he is impecunious. In civil law it is generally for the party who relies on an assertion to prove it. Second, impecuniosity arises by way of an exception to the general rule in *Dimond*. It is generally for the party who seeks to take advantage of an exception to prove that they fall within it. Third, all of the evidence related to impecuniosity is exclusively in the Claimant's possession or control. It would be ridiculous, so Defendants might argue, if the Claimant could fail to disclose this material and then benefit from this failure to disclose, because the Defendant would be unable to prove that he was not impecunious.

---

36 *Ibid*, paras 35 and 37.
37 *Ibid*, para. 37.
38 *Lagden*, para. 34.

In *W v Veolia Environmental Services UK (PLC)* HHJ Mackie QC elegantly summarised the problem which may arise: *"the burden of showing a lack of impecuniosity may rest upon the defendant but this is a matter peculiarly within the knowledge of the claimant."*[39] The Court of Appeal decision in *Umerji* resolved that problem by placing the burden of proof on the claimant in relation to impecuniosity.

Pleading

The parties should bear in mind that paragraph 8.2 of the Practice Direction to Part 16 of the Civil Procedure Rules provides in part that *"the Claimant must specifically set out the following matters in his particulars of claim if he wishes to rely on them: … (8) any facts relating to mitigation of loss or damage"*.

Claimants may argue that it is odd to require a claimant to put forwards his case on issues of mitigation before the defendant has set out his case in a defence or counter-schedule. In particular, until the defendant has evidenced the basic hire rate, it may be difficult for a claimant to say whether or not they could afford to pay the basic hire rate.

However, defendants may observe that in *Umerji*, the Court of Appeal drew attention to the Practice Direction and observed that, consistent with their conclusion that credit hire charges were expenses incurred in mitigation of the primary loss, *"the claimant should plead his case as to reasonabless, including any assertion of impecuniosity"*.[40]

Where a claimant fails to address impecuniosity in his pleadings, the defendant has two options. The defendant could make an application for a debarring order or in the alternative full disclosure / clarification of the claimant's case. Alternatively, the defendant could simply raise the issue at the end of trial in support of the submission that the claimant has failed to prove impecuniosity.

---

39 *W v Veolia*, para. 60.
40 *Umerji*, para. 13 fn. 2.

It remains unclear exactly what details the claimant should provide in the particulars of claim. Claimants may argue that it is sufficient to indicate that impecuniosity is in issue, so that the defendant knows the case that it has to meet. Defendants may respond that the Practice Direction requires the claimant to plead "any facts" relating to mitigation. That might suggest that the Claimant is required to plead the factual underpinning of any assertion of impecuniosity.

Disclosure / Part 18 Questions

Given the uncertainties inherent in the definition of impecuniosity and the risk of a claimant being able to give new information about his finances in oral evidence, it is usually beneficial for the Defendant to try to obtain clear information and disclosure about impecuniosity at an early stage. After all, in *Lagden,* Lord Nicholls suggested that *"Motor insurers and credit hire companies should be able to agree on standard enquiries, or some other means, which in practice can most readily give effect to this test of impecuniosity".*[41]

For claims that are in the fast track and multi-track, the Claimant must comply with standard disclosure. This means that he / she is obliged to disclose those documents *"on which he relies"* and which *"adversely affect his own case".*[42] Where impecuniosity is in issue, it is likely that all bank statements, wage slips, credit card statements and other financial statements will either be documents on which the claimant relies or documents which adversely affect his own case. They should therefore be disclosed. The Defendant may also request further information from the Claimant pursuant to CPR Part 18 should clarification be required.

On the small claims track, the disclosure provisions are more limited. However, the parties are still required to disclose the documents on which they rely and Civil Procedure Rule 27.2(3) additionally provides that the Court may *"order a party to provide further information if it considers it appropriate to do so".*

---

41 *Lagden,* para. 9.
42 Civil Procedure Rules 31.6.

As a result, it is likely to be difficult for the Claimant to avoid the disclosure of relevant information and documents.

Defendants should also note that the Court has the power pursuant to Civil Procedure Rule 3.1(2)(k) to *"exclude an issue from consideration"*. The Defendant may rely on this provision to invite the Court to exclude the issue of impecuniosity, where the Claimant fails to comply with disclosure (and indeed where the Claimant fails to plead his position on impecuniosity as addressed in the previous subsection).

Many Courts now issue standard form orders in credit hire cases, which require the Claimant to disclose all relevant financial statements for a fixed period (usually three months before and three months after the period of hire).

Claimants should be aware that cases have been struck out for failure to disclose the relevant documents: cf *Saeed v Ellis*.[43] In many other cases concerns about partial disclosure feature as a reason for finding against the Claimant: see for example *Singh v Aqua Descaling Ltd*.[44] The modern approach to litigation is to front-load the costs so far as possible. Consistent with that approach, it is suggested that Claimants should ideally consider the position in relation to impecuniosity before issuing proceedings – including obtaining the relevant documents. If this ground work is done, the Claimant will be well placed to plead the issue properly in the Particulars of Claim (with the aim of discouraging the Defendant from investigating rates evidence at all) and overcome any procedural hurdles.

Other Potential Exceptions to Dimond

One of the criticisms that Lord Walker advanced of the "choice" test is that it is not expressly limited to a claimant's financial resources. As Lord Walker put it:

---

43 Nicol J, High Court of Justice, Queen's Bench Division, Manchester District Registry, 4 June 2009, Unreported.

44 HHJ Oliver-Jones QC, Walsall County Court, 6 June 2008, unreported. Many more examples could be given.

"This claimant's choice was restricted by his extreme impecuniosity. The freedom of choice open to other claimants might be restricted by all sorts of other circumstances, such as the remote geographical location in which an accident occurred, the specialised character of the claimant's vehicle or a dislocation of the normal market caused by exceptional demand. The proposed modification of the principle in Dimond v Lovell seems dangerously open-ended" [45]

Defendants may well argue that *Lagden* is a narrow decision focussing on the question of impecuniosity alone. Indeed, throughout their speeches (at least the speeches in the majority) their Lordships were focussing only on the question of financial means. It is therefore misleading, so the argument runs, to submit that the judgement has any wider implications: instead, it might be said, that it creates one narrow exception only.

Claimants may respond, however, that the ratio of *Lagden* is not tied to financial means but is that if the Claimant has no choice but to hire on credit, the additional benefits that he thereby receives are purely incidental to obtaining a replacement vehicle. Thus, where freedom of choice is limited by any other factor including those described by Lord Walker, the Claimant may argue for recovery of the full credit hire rate.

In this regard, the Claimant's age is likely to be an important consideration. Many car hire companies will not hire to individuals younger than a certain age (or indeed older than a certain age), particularly where the vehicle in question is particularly powerful. Such a Claimant can argue convincingly that they had no alternative but to hire on credit and so that they should recover the credit hire charges in full. As we have already seen in Chapter One, a related argument was accepted in *Bent No2*, on the basis that the defendant's basic hire rates evidence was not truly comparable to the credit hire rate, and hence the defendant had failed to discharge the burden of proof in that regard, because none of the surveyed hire companies would actually have hired to someone of the claimant's age.

---

45 *Lagden*, para. 104.

CHAPTER THREE
MITIGATION OF LOSS

A. INTRODUCTION

A further way for Defendant Insurers to attack credit hire charges is to argue that the Claimant has failed to mitigate his loss. In short, that the Claimant has acted unreasonably.

In assessing the strength of arguments based on mitigation of loss it is important to start with a firm grip on the general principles of mitigation. We will summarise them first. In this regard, we should add one word of caution. Mitigation is a difficult subject, about which whole books have been written. This chapter is not a substitute for such works as McGregor on Damages, which contains an excellent account of the law on mitigation.

But in addition to the general principles, the practitioner also needs to be aware of the increasing volume of cases applying these general principles to credit hire scenarios. These cases are the primary focus of this chapter.

We should also note that in *Copley v Lawn*[1], the Court of Appeal expressed doubts about the application of mitigation of loss in this area:

---

1 *Copley v Lawn* and *Maden v Haller*, [2009] EWCA Civ 580 at para. 6.

"judges should, in my view, be reluctant to become too readily involved in complicated mitigation arguments since the major protection for the defendant and his insurers is that the claimant can only recover the "spot" or market rate of hire as explained in Dimond v Lovell. One rarely encounters mitigation arguments in ordinary sales of goods cases precisely because the relevant statute provides that damages are to be prima facie assessed by reference to the market value of the goods. The reason is that it is usually open to the innocent buyer or seller to go into the market to acquire other goods or dispose of the contractual goods and that is what he ought to be doing by way of mitigation of his loss. There is no reason why loss of use claims based on the hire of goods should be any different. I would, therefore, look with some scepticism on arguments that an innocent claimant should take further steps (over and above ensuring that he is not hiring a replacement car for more than the market rate) by way of mitigating his own loss or protecting the tortfeasor's position."

For a period, this suggestion that mitigation arguments should be approached with some scepticism and disappointing results for defendants in cases such as *Mattocks v Mann*, meant that the sting appeared to have been drawn out of mitigation arguments.

There has, however, been something of a resurgence of interest in mitigation in recent years. Significant Court of Appeal decisions such as *Zurich Insurance Plc v Umerji* and *Opoku v Tintas* have re-asserted the important restraint that mitigation of loss can place on excessive claims for hire charges. The net result is that mitigation arguments can no longer be lightly dismissed in this area.

B. GENERAL PRINCIPLES

It is generally accepted that Claimants should take reasonable steps to limit their losses following an accident. Thus the Claimant whose car is damaged is expected to investigate alternative means of getting to work, rather than presenting a vast claim for loss of earnings. This is usually labelled the 'duty to mitigate'.

Although this label is almost universal, even the phrase "duty to mitigate" is not without its difficulties. For a start the Claimant is not actually under an obligation to do anything at all. As Pearson LJ put it in *Darbishire v Warran*:- [2]

> "*The plaintiff is not under any actual obligation to adopt the cheaper method: if he wishes to adopt the more expensive method he is at liberty to do so and by doing so commits no wrong against the defendant or anyone else. The true meaning is that the plaintiff is not entitled to charge the defendant by way of damages with any greater sum than that which he reasonably needs to expend for the purpose of making good the loss. In short, he is fully entitled to be as extravagant as he pleases but not at the expense of the Defendant*"

The reasoning in *Darbishire v Warran* has since been strongly criticised on other grounds.[3] Nevertheless, it is submitted that the passage cited above represents the correct state of the law on mitigation; mitigation of loss is not about compelling the Claimant to take a particular course of action. It is simply about calculating what part of the Claimant's loss can be charged against the Defendant.

Burden of Proof

In previous editions of this book, we have adopted the standard analysis that the burden of proving that the Claimant acted unreasonably rests on the Defendant.

However, the Court of Appeal recently specifically addressed the burden of proof in a credit hire context in *Umerji*.[4] In that case, the Claimant had argued that whilst he bore the burden of proving impecuniosity (that he could not afford to pay basic hire rates without

---

2 [1963] 1 WLR 1067 at 1075

3 See *Coles and others v Hetherton and others* [2013] EWCA Civ 1704, at paras 30 – 31.

4 *Zurich Insurance Plc v Umerji*, [2014] EWCA Civ 357.

making unreasonable sacrifices), the Defendant bore the burden of proving that he could have afforded to purchase a replacement vehicle and so bring the period of hire to an earlier end. The issue before the Court turned on the wording of an unless order in relation to the disclosure of financial documents. But the Court went on to address the argument based on the different burdens of proof:-

> *"The correct analysis would appear to be as follows. A claim for the cost of hire of a replacement vehicle is, strictly, a claim for expenditure incurred in mitigation of the primary loss, namely the loss of use of the damaged vehicle: see the speech of Lord Hope in Lagden v O'Connor at para. 27 (p. 1077H). The burden is thus on the claimant to prove (and therefore plead) that such expenditure was reasonably incurred: see the authorities reviewed by Sir Mark Potter P in Beechwood Birmingham Ltd v Hoyer Group UK Ltd...There is no doubt a grey area about how much needs to be pleaded and proved to establish reasonableness before the evidential burden shifts to the defendant to show that the expenditure was unreasonable"[5]*

It is submitted that this analysis explains why it is often said that the Claimant bears the burden of proving that he needed to hire a replacement vehicle at all. There is an initial burden on the Claimant to show the expenditure was reasonably incurred. If the Claimant does enough to discharge that burden, then the baton passes to the Defendant to show that the Claimant nevertheless acted unreasonably.

Standard of Mitigation

The standard of mitigation has been described in different terms in different cases. Some of these formulations are more favourable to the Claimant and others to the Defendant.

Thus Claimants often rely on the purple prose of Lord MacMillan in *Banco de Portugal v Waterlow and Sons Ltd*:[6]

---

5 *Ibid*, para. 37.

6 [1932] AC 452 at 506.

"Where the sufferer from a breach of contract finds himself in consequence of that breach placed in a position of embarrassment the measures which he may be driven to adopt in order to extricate himself ought not to be weighed in nice scales at the instance of the party whose breach of contract has occasioned the difficulty. It is often easy after an emergency has passed to criticise the steps which have been taken to meet it, but such criticism does not come well from those who have themselves created the emergency. The law is satisfied if the party placed in the difficult by reason of the breach of a duty owed to him has acted reasonably in the adoption of remedial measures and he will not be held disentitled to recover the cost of such measures merely because the party in breach can suggest that other measures less burdensome to him have been taken."

Of course Lord MacMillan was speaking specifically about breach of contract. However his comments apply equally to tort. This was affirmed (for example) by Nourse LJ in *Mattocks v Mann*[7], Davies LJ in *Moore v DER*[8] and in McGregor on Damages at para. 7-70.

In borderline cases, Claimants may wish to rely on the reasoning of Sedley LJ in *Wilding v British Telecommunications.*[9] Although an employment case, the doctrine of mitigation applies equally in both jurisdictions. In that case the Respondent argued that *"you act unreasonably if you do not act reasonably"*. Sedley LJ rejected this reasoning:-

"it is not enough for the wrongdoer to show that it would have been reasonable to take the steps he has proposed: he must show that it was unreasonable of the innocent party not to take them. This is a real distinction. It reflects the fact that if there is more than one reasonable response open to the wronged party, the wrongdoer has no right to determine his choice. It is where, and only where, the wrongdoer can show affirmatively that the other party has acted

7   (1993) RTR 13 at 21E.
8   [1971] 1 WLR 1476.
9   (2002) ICR 1079.

unreasonably in relation to his duty to mitigate that the defence will succeed."[10]

On the other hand, there are other cases which suggest that the standard is wholly objective and that economic considerations may be overwhelming. Thus, Defendants may point to the following:-

"The person who has broken the contract is not to be exposed to additional cost by reason of the plaintiffs not doing what they ought to have done as reasonable men, and the plaintiffs not being under any obligation to do anything otherwise than in the ordinary course of business."[11]

A similar point was made by Pearson LJ in *Darbishire v Warran*:

"It is vital, for the purpose of assessing damages fairly between the plaintiff and the defendant, to consider whether the plaintiff's course of action 'was economic or uneconomic, and if it was uneconomic it cannot (at any rate in the absence of special circumstances, of which there is no evidence in this case) form a proper basis for assessment of damages. The question has to be considered from the point of view of a business man"[12]

The phrases the "ordinary course of business" and "economic or uneconomic" are useful for Defendants, particularly in cases where the Claimant is a company or a self -employed individual. The reason is

---

10 *Ibid*, para. 55.

11 James L.J. in *Dunkirk Colliery Co. v Lever* (1878) 9 Ch.D.20 at 25, cited with approval by Viscount Haldane in *British Westinghouse Electric and Manufacturing Co. Ltd v Underground Electric Railways Company of London Ltd* [1912] AC 673 (at 689).

12 *Darbishire v Warran*. We note that in *Coles v Hetherton*, the Court of Appeal described the discussion of mitigation in *Darbishire v Warran* as an "aberration" because the Court wrongly applied concepts of mitigation to the cost of repairing a vehicle. Although this does not mean that the description of the principles of mitigation in that case was wrong, it would be unwise to rely too heavily upon it in the light of that criticism.

that it suggests that the court should look simply at the costs of the choice made by the Claimant. This is often helpful because the high costs of credit hire often enable Defendants to argue that they are out of the "ordinary course of business" or "uneconomic".

It may also be worthwhile for the Defendant to point out that the standard of reasonableness is objective. In the classic case of *Marcroft v Scruttons Ltd*,[13] concerning a claimant's refusal to undergo medical treatment, the Court of Appeal had to consider whether the standard is objective or subjective. It held that the Court should not take into account subjective factors:-

> "*The difficult question in this case is whether we are to admit this subjective condition of his as a reason for refusing medical treatment. I think not.*"

Question of Fact

It is commonly asserted that issues of mitigation are questions of fact for the trial Judge to determine. One source for this principle is *Payzu v Saunders*:-

> "*It is plain that the question what is reasonable for a person to do in mitigation of his damages cannot be a question of law but must be one of fact in the circumstances of each particular case.*"[14]

However this statement requires qualification. It is clear that whilst questions of mitigation are still regarded as findings of fact, they are not treated in the same way as findings about, for example, the speed of a vehicle involved in a road traffic accident. Thus the Court of Appeal observed in overturning the trial Judge's findings on mitigation in *Copley v Lawn*:-

> "*There is no question of any interference with any finding of primary fact; questions of mitigation are however, questions of eval-*

13 1954 Lloyds Reports Vol. 1 395.
14 [1919] 2 KB 581 at 588.

uation and judgment and there is no reason why this court should not interfere, if the judge's conclusions are, in its considered opinion, wrong".[15]

It is submitted that this analysis is correct. Primary factual findings – for instance in a credit hire context, the date when repairs started or when the claimant became that his vehicle was a write-off – are in a different league from findings in relation to mitigation, which involve applying the test of unreasonableness to the facts. Accordingly, it is right that less deference is accorded to the findings at first instance in relation to mitigation and there is more scope for appellate intervention.

C. COMMON MITIGATION ISSUES

The scenarios addressed below are not an exhaustive list. By their nature, mitigation arguments can arise in novel factual situations, wherever the suggestion can be made that the Claimant has acted unreasonably. But questions of mitigation are particularly prone to arise in the following contexts:-

1. Need for a Hire Car
2. Courtesy Cars
3. Like for Like
4. Period of Hire
5. Self-Employed Claimants and Businesses

1. Need for a Hire Car

It is unreasonable for a Claimant to hire a replacement vehicle, if in truth he had no reason to use the replacement vehicle whilst his own was unavailable.

This flows from the general principle explained in *Umerji* and set out above, that the Claimant bears an initial burden of showing that the expense of hire charges was reasonably incurred in mitigation of the loss of use of his vehicle.

---

15 *Copley v Lawn* para. 23.

As Lord Hope explained in *Lagden*:-

> *"The motorist cannot claim for the cost of hiring another vehicle if he had no reason to use a car while his own car was being repaired – if, for example, he was in hospital during the relevant period or out of the country on a package holiday."*[16]

In fact, need for a hire car was identified as an issue in the very first credit hire case to reach the House of Lords. In *Giles v Thompson*[17], which dealt primarily with issues arising from champerty, Lord Mustill went on to give useful guidance regarding need to hire a replacement vehicle. He stated that: *"the need for a replacement car is not self-proving."* He went on to say that it was for the Defendant to *"displace the inference"* which otherwise arose.

He explained that:

> *"I agree with the Court of Appeal that it is not hard to infer that a motorist who incurs the considerable expense of running a private car does so because he has a need for it, and consequently has a need to replace it if, as a result of a wrongful act, it is put out of commission."*

Lord Mustill went on to warn against permitting exaggerated claims for car hire:

> *"What matters is that the judges should look carefully at claims for hiring, both as to their duration and as to their rate. This will do much to avoid the inflated claims of which the defendants' insurers are understandably apprehensive, and will also discourage the promotion of over-optimistic claims by motorists, who if the present forms of agreement are enforced in accordance with their terms may be left with residual liabilities for hiring charges. The discipline imposed by judges who have the acumen and experience to detect greed*

---

16 *Lagden v O'Connor,* para. 27.
17 [1994] AC 142.

and slapdash claims procedures will in my opinion do much more to forestall abuse than a dusting-down of the old law of champerty."

He continued at pages 164 -165:

"And as to the possibility that the scheme will encourage motorists to hire cars which they do not need, at the ultimate expense of the insurers, I am confident that resourceful lawyers are well able to press by interlocutory measures for a candid exposure of the motorist's true requirements, and, if all else fails, to fight the issue at an oral hearing, as happened in the present case. If the motorists are found to have been tempted by the hire companies into the unnecessary hiring of substitute vehicles, the claims will fail pro tanto, with consequent orders for costs which will impose a healthy discipline upon the companies."

Despite this warning, Lord Mustill only gave two examples of situations in which the Claimant might fail to establish need: *"The motorist may have been in hospital throughout . . . ; or he may have been planning to go abroad for a holiday leaving his car behind; and so on. . . ."*

Whilst this was plainly not intended as an exhaustive list, the examples chosen should be familiar. The very same examples were used by Lord Hope in the passage from *Lagden* set out above and in the Court of Appeal in *Giles v Thompson*[18] by Steyn LJ (as he then was).

In explaining his conclusions, Steyn LJ added that the Claimant *"clearly"* did not have to show that the car was *"essential"*. Rather *"[i]t is sufficient to show that he acted reasonably"*.[19]

These citations indicate that whilst it is correct to say that the Claimant bears an initial burden of showing that hire charges were reasonably incurred, in relation to his need to hire, this is not a heavy burden. The only examples given in the above cases of situations in which need would not be established are extreme cases – sickness or holidays. In most

18 Times, 13 January 1993, at page 337H.
19 *Ibid*, at 337G.

ordinary situations, an individual claimant is likely to be able to establish a need for a replacement vehicle.

Nevertheless, experience shows that the Defendant can successfully challenge need to hire on the facts in a variety of situations. These include situations where the Claimant had access to other vehicles through family members or business connections, or where the Claimant clearly managed without a vehicle either before or after the hire period (though here it may be on the facts that the Claimant's situation has changed).

Need and Companies

A particular difficulty sometimes arises where the Claimant is a company and the damaged vehicle is one of a number of fleet vehicles. How can such a Claimant prove that they needed to hire a replacement vehicle? If they cannot establish need, does this extinguish the claim altogether?

Establishing Need in relation to a Corporate Claimant

If a corporation intends to argue that it needed to hire a replacement vehicle, it should provide evidence to justify that need. In two significant cases, the evidence provided was inadequate with disastrous consequences for the claims.

First, in *Park Lane BMW v Whipp*,[20] HHJ Harris found that there was no need to hire, in part because the Claimant had produced no evidence of the size and utilisation of its fleet, no evidence of what either vehicle was used for or was intended to be used for and no evidence about whether there were any other vehicles available to it.

Second, in Singh v Yaqubi,[21] the Court of Appeal upheld a first instance finding that the Claimant had failed to prove a reasonable need for a replacement vehicle. In that case, the Claimant sought to recover hire charges of £99,439.06 for charges associated with two vehicles: a

---

20 *Park Lane BMW v Whipp*, HHJ Harris, unreported 20 May 2009.
21 *Singh v Yaqubi*, [2013] EWCA Civ 23.

Bentley and a Rolls Royce. In upholding the first instance decision that he had failed to establish need, the Court of Appeal said this:-

> *"Very large hire claims such as this one should be scrutinised carefully by the court and particularly when the business partnership, which was required to establish the need, had a fleet of seven prestigious cars on the same insurance. For such a business claim to succeed, the judge was entitled to require specific evidence of need, such as evidence of the actual use of the vehicle for business purposes before the accident and the use to which the hired vehicle was put during the period of hire. Such evidence as was given, was vague and non-specific and the judge was entitled to hold that the need for a replacement Rolls Royce had not been established."*[22]

It is apparent from the passages cited from the first instance decision that there were real evidential gaps in that case. The Claimant himself had been abroad for part of the hire period and could say nothing specific about the use of the hire vehicle whilst he was away; he believed it was used for moving clients around. Moreover, no work diary or equivalent document was disclosed to show the use of either the hire vehicle or (before the accident) the damaged vehicle. As a result, a claim for almost £100,000 was dismissed in its entirety.

These cases might create the impression that it is very difficult for a company with a fleet to establish need. But that is not necessarily right; it is all a question of establishing the right evidence. For example, in *R S Fleet Installations Ltd v Southern Rock Insurance Company Ltd*,[23] the Claimant called evidence from its Fleet Manager who was able to explain that all of its vehicles were already allocated to specific employees. HHJ Gregory did not hesitate to find that need was established.

It is suggested that in preparing cases, Claimants could usefully read *Singh* and *Park Lane BMW* as providing a shopping list of the evidence that is likely to be required to establish need in similar cases. Careful

---

22 Ibid, para. 39.
23 Unreported, Walsall County Court, 4 May 2014.

thought should be given to disclosure; particularly if there are documents demonstrating the utilisation of the Claimant's fleet of vehicles. Moreover, care is needed in the selection of witnesses – the driver of the vehicle may not be best placed to answer questions about the potential availability of other vehicles and an additional witness may be required to plug this gap.

Conversely, of course, Defendants should analyse the Claimant's evidence against these decisions to highlight what evidence is missing. Tactically, Defendants may wish to think carefully before putting Part 18 Questions on these issues, which, if badly drafted, might do no more than given the Claimant a second chance to put the appropriate evidence in.

What is the measure of loss if need is not established?

Suppose that a company fails to establish need on the basis that it could have re-allocated another vehicle from its fleet. Does that mean that it can recovery no damages for loss of use or that there must be some other measure of loss?

In _Beechwood Birmingham Ltd v Hoyer Group UK Ltd_,[24] this point reached the Court of Appeal on unusual facts. The Claimant was a substantial Audi dealer, with a fleet of 64 vehicles. When one of its fleet vehicles was damaged, it hired a replacement from a credit hire company. Apparently the Claimant admitted that it had no need to hire a vehicle. In other similar situations it had just re-allocated a vehicle from its fleet. Rather the evidence was that it wanted to test the efficacy of the credit hire process, in order to decide whether to refer its customers in the future. It is no surprise that at first instance there was a finding that the Claimant had no need to hire.

The Court of Appeal reviewed the authorities and concluded:-

> "_the net result of the shipping cases can be stated as follows. Where a_
> _substitute vessel is hired in to fulfil the role of the damaged vessel,_

---

24 [2010] EWCA Civ 647.

the costs of hiring in are recoverable. Where the claimant's fleet is sufficient to provide a standby, then an award may be made based upon the expenses of keeping that standby, which means not only the expenses of daily upkeep but something representing the amount of capital employed in having another ship available. Where there is no substitute ship hired and no standby ship kept available the damages awarded are generally to be calculated on the basis of interest on the capital value of the damaged ship at the time of the collision. "[25]

The Court held that cases brought by corporations for loss of use of a chattel used for the business form a distinct class of cases from those brought by private individuals. In cases involving corporations, the loss *"should be the subject of an award of such sum as reasonably compensates for the nature and extent of the financial loss suffered as a result of the neutering of the damaged vehicle as an asset employed in the claimant's business and the redeployment of any other such asset."* [26]

The Court of Appeal then discussed how best to quantify this loss. It settled on this formulation: *"an award based on the interest and capital employed and any depreciation sustained over the period of repairs, allowed in respect of the vehicle of the type damaged in the accident."* [27]

The result appears to be that:-

1. If a company can show that it needed to hire a replacement vehicle, it can recover those hire charges (subject to the usual arguments about mitigation and rate);

2. If the company's fleet was large enough to provide a standby, and hence there was no need to hire, then a more limited award should be made based on the interest and capital employed on the damaged vehicle and the cost of having a substitute available

---

25 Para. 45.

26 Para 49.

27 Para 52.

Finally, it is perhaps worth noting that in credit hire cases the Court is rarely provided with the information on which to quantify the damages in the manner suggested by the Court of Appeal. In *Beechwood Birmingham* itself, the Court of Appeal had no evidence about how to quantify the loss and hence invited the parties to agree the appropriate figure based on their guidance. The Court of Appeal noted that *"the figures produced by any further exercise on the lines I have indicated would scarcely justify the time and cost involved in further remission to the Judge"*. This was perhaps a little generous to the Claimant who had failed to provide the relevant evidence to prove this loss. Defendants might rely o n *Park Lane BMW v Whipp*, in which confronted with the same problem HHJ Harris had simply dismissed the claim for hire charges. It appears that the Claimant also recovered nothing in *Singh v Yaqubi*. Given that Claimants should now be familiar with the decision in *Beechwood Birmingham*, it is more likely that other Judge will take this course in the future should Claimants fail to provide the necessary evidence.

2. Courtesy Cars

The issue here is simple: is it reasonable for a Claimant to hire a replacement vehicle in circumstances where they have been offered a courtesy car either through their own insurance or by the Defendant?

a) From the Claimant's Own Insurer

If the Claimant's own insurer offers the Claimant a courtesy car, is it a failure to mitigate for the Claimant to take a credit hire vehicle instead?

In the late 1990s inconsistent results were reached in the County Courts on this issue.[28] However, the current state of the authorities presents a

---

28 Thus the defendant succeeded in *Callender v Ray Braidwood & Sons* [1999] 1 CL, *Bucknall v Jepson* [1998] CLY 1456, *Spence v United Taxis* [1998] CLY 1465 and *Ball v Howells Transport* [1999] CL, DJ Ackroyd and *Lyons v Metcalf* [1999] CLY 2494 (save that in *Lyons* this was *obiter* since the claim failed in any event); whereas the claimant succeeded on the same issue in *Perehenic v Deboa Structuring* [1998] CLY 1467 and *Cockburn v Davies and Provident Insurance Plc* [1997] CLY 1805.

number of obstacles in the way of the Defendant succeeding on such an argument.

The first obstacle is that Claimants may argue that benefits received under an insurance policy should be left out of account. This builds on the principle of res inter alios acta, an early account of which was given in *Bradburn v the Great Western Railway Company.*[29] The defendant sought to deduct the proceeds of an accident insurance policy from the damages to which the claimant was entitled in compensation. The Court held that the insurance policy should be left out of account. Pigott B explained:

> *"He [the claimant] does not receive that sum of money because of the accident, but because he has made a contract providing for the contingency; an accident must occur to entitle him to it, but it is not the accident, but his contract, which is the cause of his receiving it"*

The same point was picked up in *Parry v Cleaver.*[30] This case is familiar to personal injury lawyers as it holds that payments that the Claimant has received from occupational disability pensions do not have to be deducted from his damages. In so holding, Lord Reid stated at page 14:

> *"As regards moneys coming to the plaintiff under a contract of insurance, I think that the real and substantial reason for disregarding them is that the plaintiff has bought them and that it would be unjust and unreasonable to hold that the money which he has prudently spent on premiums and the benefit from it should enure to the benefit of the tortfeasor. Here again I think that the explanation that this is too remote is artificial and unreal. Why should the plaintiff be left worse off than if he had never insured?"*

This result was applied in a credit hire context by HHJ Harris in *Seddon v Tekin.*[31] HHJ Harris stated that *"There is no reason why a Defendant should be able to take advantage of the fact that the plaintiff is insured to reduce his own loss."* This is entirely consistent with *Parry v Cleaver.* But

---

29 (1874) LR 10 Ex 1.
30 [1970] AC 1.
31 [2001] GCCR 2865.

HHJ Harris also gave a further reason: *"and if the plaintiff did so by taking the car from his own insurer then his own insurer could recover the cost from the Defendant anyway, so the defendant's position would not be improved"*.

This line of authority was also considered in *Rose v the Co-operative Group*,[32] in which the Circuit Judge concluded *"whether or not the Claimant knew or ought to have known he had a choice of car free of charge through his own insurance, the availability of such a choice by use of his own insurance should be disregarded."*

This suggests that Claimants may be able to argue that as a matter of principle any benefits coming to the Claimant under a contract of insurance (including a courtesy car) should be left out of account in assessing damages. This would be fatal to any contention that the Claimant failed to mitigate by failing to take a courtesy car.

The second obstacle is that there is a line of authority suggesting that where the Claimant has a choice between recovering from the Defendant and recovering from another source (for example, their own insurer), it is generally not unreasonable to look to recover the loss from the Defendant in the first instance.

In *Martindale v Duncan*,[33] the Court of Appeal held that on the facts of that case it was not a failure to mitigate for the Claimant to seek to recover damages from the Defendant in the first instance rather than his own insurer. Davies LJ said at page 577:

> *"The plaintiff was seeking in the first instance to recover his damage from the defendant's insurers and, if anything went wrong with that claim, although he obviously would not want to forfeit his "no claims" bonus, the second string to his bow would be to recover the money from his own insurers, and until he had had authorisation for doing the work he could not be at all certain that he would stand in a good position vis-a-vis the insurance company."*

---

32 Unreported 7 February 2005.

33 [1973] 1 WLR 547.

The Court of Appeal went on to hold that it was not a failure to mitigate on the facts of that case for the Claimant to seek to recover damages in the first instance from the Defendant's insurers rather than claiming against his own insurers.

This line of argument is also be supported by *the Liverpool (No 2)*.[34] In that case, the Court of Appeal held that where the victim of an accident has differing and alternative rights for the same loss against a tortfeasor and against another in contract he is not required to take steps to recover his loss from the other party from whom he could recover in contract.

The *Liverpool No2* was recently discussed and reaffirmed by the Court of Appeal in *Peters v East Midlands Strategic Health Authority*.[35] In that personal injury case, the Defendant argued that rather than claiming the cost of care from the Defendant, the Claimant should make use of NHS care, which the local authority was under a statutory duty to provide. This argument was rejected in these terms:

> "*we can see no reason in policy or principle which requires us to hold that a claimant who wishes to opt for self-funding and damages in preference to reliance on the statutory obligations of a public authority should not be entitled to do so as a matter of right*".[36]

Claimants may also refer to the judgment of Nicholson LJ in *McMullen v Gibney and Bibney*[37] sitting in the High Court of Northern Ireland, which also held that the availability of a courtesy car to a claimant under a policy of insurance afforded no defence to a claim for hire of a replacement vehicle.

As the law currently stands, these lines of authority undoubtedly make it difficult for the Defendant to show that the Claimant failed to mit-

---

34 [1963] P64.

35 (2009) EWCA Civ 145.

36 Paragraph 53.

37 [1999] NIQB 1 (13 January 1999)

igate by failing to take advantage of a courtesy car from his own insurer. Nevertheless, in a credit hire context the point has not been definitively ruled out by the Court of Appeal. Indeed, in *Zurich Insurance Plc v Umerji*, when the Defendant sought to run this very issue, the Court of Appeal did not dismiss it out of hand. Instead, it indicated that the issue was "an interesting one and plainly of some general importance". But in that case the issue had not been pursued at first instance and accordingly the Court of Appeal concluded that "this battle will have to be fought, if insurers are so inclined, on another field".[38] Defendants might take some encouragement from the fact that the Court of Appeal did not dismiss the attempt to distinguish *Bradburn* out of hand. On appropriate facts, it plainly remains open to the Defendant to argue that it was unreasonable for the Claimant not to take a courtesy car from his own insurer – though the Defendant may need to be prepared to take the point to the Court of Appeal in order to get a full hearing on the issues.

To these principled objections, we might add that the Defendant is likely to face certain factual difficulties. It would be necessary to investigate the terms and conditions of the Claimant's insurance policy. In particular: would taking a courtesy car entail the loss of a no-claims bonus; what types of courtesy car were available to the Claimant.

b) From Defendant's Insurer

Different issues arise where the Defendant offered to provide the Claimant with a replacement vehicle. After skirmishes in the County Courts, these issues were addressed by the Court of Appeal in two important cases: *Copley v Lawn* and *Sayce v TNT*.[39]

In *Copley*, the Defendant's Insurer had written to the Claimant to offer to provide her with a courtesy car. However the letter did not specify the cost to the Defendant of providing the courtesy car. The Court of Appeal held that in these circumstances there could be no failure to mitigate. The cost to the Defendant might have been greater than the

---

38 Zurich Insurance Plc v Umerji, para. 43.
39 Copley v Lawn; Sayce v TNT [2012] 1 WLR 1261.

cost of credit hire and, if it was, it could not be unreasonable for the Claimant to choose the cheaper option. Until the Claimant was informed of the cost, there could therefore be no failure to mitigate.

The ratio of *Copley* was discussed in detail in *Sayce v TNT*. In that subsequent case, a differently constituted Court of Appeal found that the ratio of *Copley* was that:-

> *"the claimant cannot be found to have acted unreasonably in refusing the defendant's offer unless he has been made aware that by doing so he would impose a greater burden on the defendant".*[40]

Defendants should also note that the Court of Appeal were critical of the drafting of the intervention letter. They remarked that it had *"an unpleasant threatening tone"* and that it was *"tempting"* to find that the claimant was entitled to *"ignore it completely"*.[41] Intervention letters must be carefully crafted to avoid this impression in future. Furthermore, both in *Copley* and in *Sayce* (per Pill LJ) the Court was particularly critical of the practice of Defendant Insurers cold-calling the Claimant.[42]

The Court of Appeal in *Copley* went on to consider what the position would have been, had the offer letter specified the cost to the insurer of providing the replacement vehicle. Here the conclusion was less clear. The Court of Appeal accepted that:-

> *if a defendant or his insurers does make an offer of a replacement car to an innocent claimant and he makes clear that he is going to pay less for such a car than the claimant is intending to pay (or is paying) for a car from a company such as Helphire, then (other things being equal) it may well be the case that a claimant should accept that lower cost replacement.*[43]

---

40 *Sayce*, para. 20.
41 *Copley*, para. 9.
42 *Copley*, para. 9 and *Sayce*, para. 45.
43 *Copley*, para. 22.

Defendants may argue that this suggests that, providing a simple alteration is made to the offer letter so that it specifies the cost, there is a failure to mitigate. Claimants may respond, however, that the Court of Appeal stopped short of saying that in those situations there would be a failure to mitigate. Instead it said that there "*may*" be a failure to mitigate "other things being equal". This must mean that, depending on the circumstances of the case, there might not be a failure to mitigate.

In *Copley*, the Court of Appeal did not discuss the question of reasonableness in any further detail. But the point arose again in *Sayce v TNT*. The procedural history of *Sayce* was deeply unusual, because in it HHJ Harris had declined to follow the Court of Appeal decision in *Copley*. Strictly, to dispose of the appeal it was sufficient to note that by the doctrine of precedent, the circuit Judge was bound to follow the Court of Appeal decision.[44] But one member of the Court of Appeal went on to express views about whether it would be unreasonable for a Claimant to refuse an offer in these circumstances.

Lord Justice Pill, delivering a separate concurring opinion,[45] noted that in assessing the reasonableness of the Claimant's refusal of the Defendant's offer, the following might be relevant considerations on the facts:-

- Whether the Claimant is given a reasonable time to consider their position;

- Whether the insurance cover to be provided accords with the victim's existing insurance arrangements in terms of additional drivers or unusual drivers;

- Whether the victim prefers to deal with a company in which they have confidence rather than the defendant's insurer.

These sort of considerations led Lord Justice Pill to remark that in the offer letter the Defendant "*may need to descend to particulars*". This suggests

---

44 *Sayce*, paras 22 and 24.
45 *Sayce*, paras 46-48.

that even where the Defendant offers to provide a vehicle and specifies the cost, there is ample scope for the Claimant to argue that it was nevertheless reasonable to refuse the offer on the facts of particular cases. Nor are the Claimant's arguments necessarily limited to those itemised by Pill LJ. For example, the Claimant might wish to challenge whether the vehicle provided by the Defendant was really an equivalent vehicle. Defendants may take some comfort from the fact that the other two Court of Appeal judges in *Sayce* did not associate themselves with this reasoning.

The Court of Appeal returned to the reasoning in *Copley* on a further occasion in *Manton Hire & Sales Ltd.*[46] In the context of the very different facts of that case, the Court observed that Copley was *"an unusual case"* because where a motorist is seeking an alternative vehicle *"time is of the essence in that the motorist will often if not usually need to make arrangements for a replacement vehicle as a matter of urgency"*. In that context, the Court of Appeal suggested that the Defendant may realistically have *"only one chance"* to make an intervention offer.[47] That suggests that in the assessment of reasonableness in a credit hire case, the timing of the offer is likely to be a critical factor.

The next question which arises is whether the Claimant is entitled to recover anything by way of damages, if he has unreasonably refused the offer of a vehicle from the Defendant. In *Copley*, the Court of Appeal concluded that:

> *"if a claimant does unreasonably reject or ignore a defendant's offer of a replacement car, the claimant is entitled to recover at least the cost which the defendant can show he would reasonably have incurred; he does not forfeit his damages claim altogether"*[48]

In other words, the Claimant should recover the amount that it would have cost the Defendant to provide the courtesy vehicle.

---

46 *Manton Hire & Sales Ltd v Ash Manor Cheese Company Ltd,* [2013] EWCA Civ 548.

47 *Ibid.,* para. 38.

48 *Copley,* para. 32.

This conclusion has proved controversial. It provoked HHJ Harris to depart from the Court of Appeal's decision in *Sayce*. Even though the Court of Appeal in *Sayce* found that HHJ Harris was bound to follow *Copley*, the majority (Moore-Bick LJ with Aitkens LJ agreeing) were critical of the Court of Appeal's reasoning. A plain reading of Moore-Bick LJ's judgment is enough to identify his doubts:-

> *"I can understand why some find it difficult to see why the claimant should be entitled to recover anything…I respectfully question whether the analogy with the offer of money is sound [which the Court in Copley had relied on]…I would respectfully doubt whether Strutt v Whitnell supports the conclusion for which it was cited… I confess that I also have difficulty with the conclusion that a claimant who has unreasonably refused an offer from the defendant of a free car can recover "at least the cost which the defendant can show he [i.e. the defendant] would reasonably have incurred" (paragraph 32). That, it seems to me, reflects the approach taken in the first part of the judgment, namely that one must look at the matter from the defendant's point of view, but it is not an approach that is reflected in the earlier authorities. Nor, with respect, do I think that it is one that is easy to reconcile with the principle relating to avoidable loss to be derived from the leading cases and summarised in McGregor on Damages 18th ed., paragraphs 7-004 and 7-014"* [49]

It is difficult to recall another Court of Appeal decision which has been so openly critical of the reasoning of another (not much) earlier Court of Appeal decision, without actually departing from it. In *Sayce* permission to appeal to the Supreme Court was refused, in part because an appeal could only be academic for the result of that case. But this does not mean the point is forever closed. The divisions in the Court of Appeal suggest that there is an opportunity for Defendants to run this point, perhaps all the way to the Supreme Court.

It is worth noting that this is a point of general importance not limited to credit hire cases: for example, would it be unreasonable for a Claimant in a personal injury case to arrange their own physiotherapy rather than use a

---

49 *Sayce*, paras 27 – 28.

physiotherapist paid by the Defendant? This suggests that clarification would benefit the law of damages as a whole.

One further oddity in the decision in *Copley* is that the Court of Appeal considered *"the extent to which (if at all) it is right to take account of the fact that both parties are insured"*.[50] The Court noted that at first instance the Judges had conflated the position of the Claimants and their respective insurers and solicitors. The Court held that *"in most cases that will be the right approach"*.[51]

If this is correct, then it is open to Defendants in all mitigation cases to argue that the Court should not consider the position of the Claimant in isolation but should consider *"the combined position of the claimants and their advisers"*. This might enable Defendants to argue for a more exacting standard – what is reasonable for a lay person might be less reasonable for an insurer / solicitor well versed in the duty to mitigate. However, it should be noted that in *W v Veolia* the High Court doubted that *Copley* intended such a result: *"If the court had intended to make as fundamental a change to the law of mitigation ... the matter would have been addressed explicitly and at a greater length."*[52]

Thus to summarise the section, the only safe conclusion is that the present state of the law is that:-

a) if the Defendant offers the Claimant a courtesy vehicle without stating the cost of the vehicle to the Defendant, it is not unreasonable to refuse it;

b) if the Defendant offers the Claimant a courtesy vehicle and does state the cost of the vehicle to the Defendant, it might be unreasonable to refuse it, depending on the facts;

c) if it was unreasonable, the Claimant would still be entitled to recover the cost to the Defendant of providing the replacement.

---

50 *Copley*, para. 12.
51 *Copley*, para. 16.
52 [2012] 1 All ER Comm 667 para. 39.

3. Like for Like

Is a Claimant who drives a particular vehicle entitled to hire the same or an equivalent vehicle? Or should he, in mitigation of his loss, accept a lesser vehicle? The question often arises particularly in respect of Claimants who drive so called prestige cars such as BMWs or Mercedes.

Different cases have again reached inconsistent results on this point. Like for like was allowed or the principle assumed or accepted in: *Watson Norie Ltd v Shaw;*[53] *Mattocks v Mann;*[54] *H L Motorworks v Alwabi;*[55] *Daily Office Cleaning Contractors v Shefford;*[56] *Williams v Hoggins;*[57] *Vaughan Transport Systems v Fackrell*[58] and more recently *Brain v Yorkshire Rider Ltd.*[59] However cases in which like for like hiring was held to be unreasonable include: *Lyne v Cawley*[60] and *Gowen v Owens Radio and TV.*[61]

In *H L Motorworks v Alwabi*, a Rolls Royce was the vehicle damaged. Cairns LJ held that:

> "On the face of it, the customer was entitled to have, during the 11 days for which he was deprived of his Rolls Royce, another Rolls Royce to take its place. If it could have been shown that the amount of use he wished to make of the car in those 11 days was very small or that some other car would have been equally suitable for his purpose, then it may well be that the plaintiff company should not have met his full claim, or, if they did, would not have been entitled to pass on the claim to the defendant. But those matters, I apprehend, would be for the defendant to establish"

53 [1967] 111 Sol Jo 117.

54 [1993] RTR 13.

55 [1977] RTR 276

56 [1977] RTR 361.

57 [1996] CLY 2148.

58 [1997] CLY 1810.

59 Unreported, HHJ Grenfell, 26 March 2007.

60 [1995] CLY 1624.

61 [1995] CLY 1631.

In *Burdis v Livsey*, the Court of Appeal concluded on this issue at paragraph 133: *"if a need for a particular replacement car is established, then the cost incurred of hiring that car is recoverable."* Defendants may say that this appears to place the burden of proof on the Claimant, at least to establish a *prima facie* case of need for a particular vehicle. Claimants may point to the very low threshold for establishing need set out by Lord Mustill in *Giles v Thompson* (cited at the start of this chapter).

In *Bent (no2)*, the Court of Appeal summarised the earlier authorities:-

> *"The injured party cannot claim reimbursement for expenditure that is unreasonable. If the defendant can show that the cost that was incurred was more than was reasonable, either by proving that the claimant had no use for a replacement car in part or at all, or because the car hired was bigger or better than was reasonable in the circumstances, the amount expended on the hire must be reduced to the amount that would have been needed to hire the equivalent to the damaged car."*[62]

Two recent cases raised this issue. In *Chatterton v AXA Corporate Solutions*,[63] having reviewed the authorities, HHJ Rawlings concluded that the Claimant "is entitled to recover hire costs of a car to fulfil the reasonable transport needs of [the Claimant] and his family".[64] On the facts of that case, no doubt influenced by the answers given by the Claimant in cross-examination, the Court concluded that his reasonable needs would have been met by a standard class vehicle rather than a Mercedes / BMW. The opposite result was reached in *Gow v NFU Mutual Insurance*,[65] in which whilst acknowledging the difficulty of the issue, HHJ Bailey concluded that the Claimant had established a personal need for a like for like replacement for his Mclaren supercar. The Court summed up: "I have no doubt, having seen him in the witness box, that when Mr Gow sits in his Mclaren and drives about, even if it is only to visit a public house, he feels

---

62 *Bent* no2, para. 32.

63 Unreported, Stoke on Trent County Court, 4 August 2016.

64 *Ibid.*, para. 34.

65 Unreported, Central London County Court, 24 May 2016.

very much better in himself. I leave it at that. He does, in my judgment, establish need."[66]

The result appears to be that the choice of replacement vehicle is a question of reasonableness, to be determined on the facts of any given case.

An interesting issue arises where the Claimant's vehicle is a very old prestige vehicle with correspondingly low value and he hires a new prestige vehicle. The Defendant may argue that it was unreasonable for such a Claimant to hire what is in reality a very much more expensive vehicle. There is some support for this in the ABI General Terms of Agreement which suggests that *"Where the vehicle is over 6 years old it is the exception, rather than the rule, that a similar prestige replacement is required"*.[67] However, as set out in Chapter One in relation to rates, the Courts are unlikely to take account of the General Terms of Agreement in hostile litigation. Instead the point is likely to depend on the facts of the case. Defendants intending to run this argument should note that in order to stand any chance of success they would need to provide evidence of the cost of hiring a vehicle that the Defendant suggests is a real equivalent.

Beyond this, when the courts are called upon to adjudicate on rates evidence they will often have to determine what represents an equivalent vehicle and evidence may well be led on this issue, as set out in the Chapter on Rates Evidence above.

Finally, it is worth noting that if the car that was damaged was a sports car but in fact the Claimant only hired an ordinary car, he can only recover the rate charged for the ordinary car not the notional cost of hiring an equivalent vehicle. In *Burdis v Livsey*, one of the Claimants had his sports car damaged in an accident. He only hired a saloon as a replacement which was cheaper than a sports car would have been. The Court of Appeal held that:

---

66 *Ibid.*, para. 33.
67 Associated of British Insurers General Terms of Agreement, para 4.5.

"In the present case the loss suffered by Mr Dennard was the cost he had to pay for hire of the Vectra, not the amount which he might have paid for the hire of another car. A person who has no need for a replacement car because, for instance, he is abroad during the repair cannot recover the cost of hiring a replacement which he never incurs (see Giles v Thompson at 167D). Similarly, a person who does not incur the cost of hiring a sports car cannot recover more than the cost actually incurred."[68]

4. Period of Hire

Defendants often argue that the period of hire was unreasonable and that they should not be responsible for paying for the whole of that period. Much depends on the reason why the period of hire was prolonged.

a. Delay by Garage in Repairing the Claimant's car

Experience suggests that this is one of the most common problems in credit hire cases. Imagine, by way of example, that, in spite of an expert report from an engineer indicating that repairs to the Claimant's vehicle should take no more than three days, repairs actually take thirty days, throughout which the Claimant hired a replacement vehicle. Should he be able to recover hire charges for a period of 30 days or only for 3 day?

In *Mattocks v Mann,*[69] the Court of Appeal had to consider a case in which there had been a delay in repairing the Claimant's car. Bedlam LJ giving the leading judgment held that:

"For a supervening cause or a failure to mitigate to relieve a Defendant of a period of hire there must, in my judgment, be a finding of some conduct on her [Mrs Mattocks] part or on the part of someone for whom she is in law responsible, or indeed of a third party, which can truly be said to be an independent cause of loss of her car for that period."

---

68 *Burdis v Livsey*, para. 133.
69 [1973] RTR 13.

In *Mattocks*, this led the Court of Appeal to allow the Claimant to recover hire charges during periods of time where: (1) the garage had not yet sent the car to the repair shop; (2) the repairs took longer than expected; and (3) the garage used its *lien* to refuse to return the vehicle for four months after repairs were completed until it was paid for the repairs.

In part, these conclusions were reached because there was no evidence that the Claimant had caused the delay in sending the car to the repair shop: *"the plaintiff had put the car with reputable and well known repairers. She was not, in my view, to be criticised because they were overworked"*. In relation to the delay in repairs, the Court noted that *"there was no evidence... that the car could have been more speedily repaired elsewhere"* and was prepared to take into account that parts need to be obtained.

In *Burdis v Livsey*, the Court of Appeal expressly approved the earlier decision in *Mattocks*.[70] The Court of Appeal concluded at paragraph 121:

> *"The defendants' actions damaged the cars of Mrs Clark and Mr Dennard. They should pay the loss caused by their actions. The actual loss incurred involved hire of replacement cars for 10 days in the case of Mrs Clark and 12 days in the case of Mr Dennard. They both appear to have acted reasonably in placing the cars in the hands of respectable repairers and there were no supervening events. Further delays of that order were foreseeable. The extra loss caused by the delay in the repair must fall on the tortfeasor as there was no failure to mitigate. On the findings of fact in those cases the cost of hire should not have been reduced.'*

Thus where the Claimant's car takes an unexpectedly long time to repair, provided that the car was entrusted to an apparently reasonable repairer, the Defendant will remain liable for the whole hire period

---

70 See also a privy council decision *Candlewood Navigation Corporation Ltd v Mitsui O.S.K. Lines Ltd* [1986] 1 AC 1.

unless the Defendant can point to a <u>supervening event which was a</u> <u>independent cause of the loss of use of the car for that period</u>. Examples of such a supervening event might arise where the garage negligently causes further damage to the car whilst it is being repaired, which delays the completion of repairs. But it also means that in many more common situations, for instance where there is a delay in the garage obtaining parts, the Defendant is likely to remain liable.

This places Defendants in a difficult position. Experience suggests that there are very many credit hire cases in which the duration of repairs turns out to be very much longer than the initial estimate. Often the reason for the delay is unclear. On the Court of Appeal's analysis, there is often no proper basis for a reduction in the period of hire in these cases. The Court of Appeal's solution to the potential unfairness that this creates was to suggest: *'The insurers of the defendants should seek a contribution from the repairers for any unjustified length of repair.'*[71] As we will see, it is in fact open to serious doubt whether the Defendant can claim a contribution from the repairer. It is suggested that this might place some doubt on the correctness of the Court of Appeal's decision as a whole, because it leaves the Defendant with so little protection in cases where there is a delay in carrying out repairs.

One interesting recent case, in which the Court found a way around this problem *was Chatterton v AXA Corporate Solutions*. In that case, the Court held that contrary to the Claimant's engineering evidence the Claimant's Ford Transit van was driveable and roadworthy. He therefore had no need for a replacement vehicle until arrangements had been made for repairs to commence, which reduced the hire period to a mere 6 days. In dealing with engineering evidence which had suggested it was unroadworthy, the Court held that the engineer's action in wrongly assessing that the vehicle was unroadworthy broke the chain of causation between the Defendant's negligence and the hire charges.[72]

---

71 *Burdis v Livsey,* para. 121.

72 *Chatterton v AXA Corporate Solutions*, paras 15-23.

b. Claiming a Contribution from the Garage

Section 1(1) of the Civil Liability (Contribution) Act 1978 provides as follows:

> *"Subject to the following provisions of this section, any person liable in respect of any damage suffered by another person may recover contribution from any other person liable in respect of the same damage (whether jointly or otherwise)."*

In order to claim a contribution from another defendant pursuant to this section, it is thus a pre-requisite that both defendants are liable in respect of *the same damage*.

In *Mason v TNT*,[73] concerning a contribution claim against an insurer, HHJ Harris asked whether the insurer's potential breach of contract was "the same damage". He held that the Defendant had negligently damaged the Claimant's car. The Insurer had, possibly, breached the contract of insurance. In reliance on *Royal Brompton Hospital v Hammond*[74] he concluded that this was not the same damage:-

> *"The insurer has no responsibility at all for causing the diminution of the value of the claimant's car, nor for the need for a replacement vehicle while repairs are carried out. This was the loss or damage which the defendant caused. All that could be said against the third party is that it failed to provide some benefits which, to an extent, would have alleviated the position in which the plaintiff found herself..."*

Although that case related to a claim for contribution against an insurer, the same logic would apply to a claim for contribution against a garage. It remains possible for Defendants to argue that *Mason v TNT* represents an overly narrow reading of the words "the same damage" or that it is inconsistent with the Court of Appeal's intention in *Burdis v Livsey*. But at least at first instance, courts are likely to find the decision

---

73 Unreported, HHJ Harris, 13 March 2009.
74 [2002] 1 WLR 1397.

in *Mason* highly persuasive and this may lead to claims for contribution being struck out altogether.

Should Defendants be able to surmount this hurdle, it would be necessary to consider whether the Claimant would have a viable claim against the garage. Where the Claimant contracted directly with the garage, the position is likely to be more straightforward. But even where the contractual arrangements were not directly between the garage and the Claimant, the Courts may be persuaded to imply a duty of care between them.

In these cases, the duty the garage owes to the Claimant is inevitably fact sensitive. However in *Charnock v Liverpool Corporation,*[75] the Court of Appeal held that where the owner of a car took it to a garage for repair, on the basis that his insurers would pay the cost of the repairs pursuant to an estimate which they had accepted, the proper inference was that there was a contract between the car owner and garage to repair the car at a price acceptable to the insurers within a reasonable time and also a contract between the garage and the insurers. Accordingly, they went on, there was a contract between the car owner and the garage to repair the car within a reasonable time. This suggests that the court is likely to imply a term between Claimant and garage that repairs be completed within reasonable time.

Having established that there was an express or implied contractual term requiring repairs to be effected in a reasonable time, the next question is how high the standard of care should be. Does the garage have to act in the same manner as a reasonable body of professional garages, by analogy with the medical negligence case law? Is the garage required to complete repairs within reasonable time or with reasonable expedition? The difference is that reasonable time simply refers to the passage of time whereas expedition puts the focus onto the garage's actions. There are no clear answers to these questions yet. I n *Charnock* the court applied the standard of the "average competent repairer." It is clear however that there is not an implied term

---

75 [1968] 1 WLR 1498.

that the repairs will be completed in accordance with the time estimate: this would not be commercially realistic.

Whether or not repairs have been completed within reasonable time / with reasonable expedition is a question of fact which will depend on the circumstances of the case.

c. Claiming a Contribution from the Claimant's Insurer

Claiming a contribution from the Claimant's Insurer is likely to be very difficult.

As set out above, Defendants face a preliminary hurdle in showing that the Insurer is liable for the same damage. As set out above, current authority suggests that it is not; *Mason v TNT* itself was a case concerning a claim for contribution against an insurer.

In any event, the Defendant would face additional challenges in claiming a contribution from the Claimant's insurer. To succeed, the Defendant would need to show that the Claimant could successfully claim damages against their own insurer. This would entail:

i. showing that there was an express / implied term in the Claimant's insurance contract stating that the insurer will act with reasonable expedition;

ii. showing that there is an action for consequential losses as a result of breaching such a term;

iii. showing on the facts that the insurer breached the term and that the breach caused the Claimant loss.

In the absence of an express term stating that the insurer will handle claims efficiently and in default will be liable for consequential losses (and we are not aware of any insurance contracts with such an express term), the Defendant can only argue that there is an implied term in

the insurance contract that the insurer will act with reasonable expedition.

Different cases have reached different results in relation to whether such
an implied term exists in an insurance contract. In *Insurance Corporation of the Channel Islands v McHugh (No 1)*,[76] Mance J held that an
insurer does not owe an implied duty to conduct negotiations, assess the
amount due or make payment within a reasonable time. He considered
that such a term could not be implied either as a matter of business
efficacy or as a matter of mutual intention. However, the opposite result
was reached in *Mason v TNT*, where HHJ Harris said (obiter) that *"I
would however make clear my view that where the third party insurer
enters into a contractual obligation to repair the car, and it proceeds to get
these repairs carried out, in my judgment, it cannot sensibly assert that it
was under no obligation to get the work done within a reasonable time...
An implied term that the work would be done with a reasonable time or as
soon as reasonably practicable is clearly necessary to give efficacy to the contract."*[77]

Furthermore, the present position is that an insured cannot recover
damages for consequential losses arising out of late payment of an
insurance claim. The reason is that the insurer is liable to indemnify the
insured from the moment of loss. It is therefore liable in damages from
that moment. The only remedy for late payment of damages is interest,
because it is not possible to recover further damages for losses arising
out of the late payment of damages. Where an insurer delays paying a
claim, the only remedy available to the insured is interest. Relevant
caselaw includes *Sprung v Royal Insurance* among others.[78]

It is also not possible to claim damages for inconvenience or distress
arising out of late payment of insurance claims. The reasons are, first,

---

76 [1997] LRLR 94.

77 *Mason v TNT*, para. 26.

78 [1999] Lloyds Rep IR 111 followed in *Tonkin v UK Insurance Ltd* [2006]
EWHC 1120 TCC.

that an insurance contract is not considered a contract to secure peace of mind and, second, that the only remedy for late payment is interest.[79]

Thus the law at present stands against the Defendant. It would take a House of Lords decision or Parliament to reform the law. However, there are signs that change might be forthcoming. The Court of Appeal in *Mandrake Holding Ltd v Countrywide Assurance Group Plc*[80] indicated that the House of Lords might revisit the law in this area. Similarly concerns have been expressed in a 2006 Law Commission report and in academic articles about the state of the law in this area.

There may also be a specific clause in the insurance policy excluding liability for consequential loss. Depending on the precise wording of the exclusion clause, this might operate to limit liability for breach of any implied term.

If the Defendant succeeds in establishing that there was such an implied term in the Claimant's insurance policy, it would then have to establish that the insurer breached that term and that the breach caused the Claimant increased loss. This will inevitably be fact sensitive. It is unlikely that every administrative delay would be held to be a breach of contract: the courts would be sensitive to commercial realities. Clearly the Defendant's argument becomes more attractive the more severe the delay. Further there is a practical difficulty for Defendants in that all the evidence about the alleged delay would be held by the Claimant's insurer.

d. Delay in Replacing or Starting Repairs to the Claimant's vehicle

Issues relating to the period of hire may also arise either where the Claimant's vehicle is written off in the accident or where the Claimant delays in instructing a garage to start repairs to his vehicle (this is different from (a) above because the delay is on the part of the Claimant himself). In these situations, one issue is often whether the Claimant can afford to replace / repair his vehicle. Claimants often hire a vehicle

---

79 See, for instance, *Ventouris v Mountain* [1992] 2 Lloyds Rep 281.

80 [2005] EWCA civ 840.

until the Defendant Insurer refunds them the pre-accident value of the vehicle to enable them to purchase a new vehicle or pays the cost of repairs. If this results in an unduly long period of hire (more than 12 months is not unknown), is there likely to be a failure to mitigate?

These issues have been explored in two recent Court of Appeal cases. In *Zurich Insurance Plc v Umerji*, the Claimant's vehicle which was damaged in the accident was a Mercedes worth around £8,000. The accident occurred in October 2010. The Mercedes was not driveable. In early November 2010, the Claimant received an engineer's report suggesting that it was a write off. He did not receive a cheque for the pre-accident value of the vehicle from the Defendant until November 2012. In the interim, he had hired a replacement vehicle on credit for 591 days at a total cost of roughly £95,000. He argued that he could not have afforded to replace his vehicle until the Defendant paid him its pre-accident value.[81]

As explained in Chapter 2 above, the Court of Appeal began by holding that a debarring order in relation to impecuniosity applied just as much in relation to period of hire as it did in relation to rates. That meant that the Claimant was debarred from asserting that he could not have afforded to replace his vehicle.[82]

The Court of Appeal held:-

pecurious

> *"the Claimant was indeed debarred from asserting that he could not afford to buy a replacement vehicle. It follows that he should only have been entitled to recover hire charges up to the date when he should reasonably have done so."*[83]

period

On the facts, the Court of Appeal concluded that it was reasonable for the Claimant to wait until his vehicle had been assessed by an engineer to see if repairs were practicable AND to wait until the Defendant "had had the opportunity to inspect it and say whether they agreed". In

---

81 See the facts summarised in *Umerji*, paras 1-2.

82 *Umerji*, paras 37-39.

83 *Ibid.*, para. 39.

Umerji, the Defendant did not indicate whether it intended to inspect and the Claimant disposed of the vehicle in mid February 2011. The Court of Appeal held that *"it was reasonable for the Claimant to wait until that date before deciding to go ahead and buy a replacement. He could have bought a replacement vehicle within a fortnight thereafter".*[84]

On its face, *Umerji* is thus a strong endorsement of the principle that a pecunious Claimant cannot reasonably continue to run up hire charges until paid the pre-accident value by an Insurer.

Claimants may note, however, that the Court of Appeal did not hold that the Claimant should have replaced his own vehicle immediately or even within fourteen days of receipt of his engineering evidence. Instead, he was allowed to wait until the Defendant had a chance to clarify its position. That resulted in hire charges being allowed from 20 October 2010 – 8 March 2011, a period of some four and a half months which is not insubstantial.

That in turn suggests that the Defendant should clarify its position at an early stage. If the Defendant had written to the Claimant to indicate that (1) liability was disputed and so no payment will be made for pre-accident value and (2) the Defendant had no intention of inspecting the vehicle, the period of hire permitted in *Umerji* might have been significantly shorter.

Logically, the same result should apply to cases in which the Claimant delays in instructing a garage to repair his vehicle. Indeed, HHJ Gregory reached an analogous result in *R S Fleet Installations Ltd*, holding that *"in permitting the matter to drift...in failing to take steps either to repair the car or have it replaced I am satisfied that a company of the size and scale with the assets of RS Fleet Installations Ltd failed to mitigate its loss."*[85]

---

84 *Ibid.*, para. 40.

85 RS Fleet Installations Ltd v Southern Rock Insurance Company Ltd, HHJ Gregory, Walsall County Court, 4 May 2014 at para. 14.

That, of course, leaves open the position of the impecunious Claimant. The law cannot expect the Claimant to do the impossible and so, if a Claimant really could not afford to repair or replace the vehicle, it may be that there is no failure to mitigate. However, just because a Claimant could not afford to repair / replace the vehicle at the start of the hire period does not mean that he remained so throughout. In *Opoku v Tintas*,[86] the Claimant sought to recover credit hire charges of roughly £130,000 incurred over a period of almost two years on the basis that he could not have afforded to pay for repairs, which were estimated to cost roughly £3,400. It was held at first instance that he was indeed impecunious in relation to hire charges. But, the Court held that a point came when he should nevertheless have paid for repairs. The Claimant appealed on the basis that this was inconsistent with the finding in relation to impecuniosity.

The Court of Appeal began by noting that "in the context of credit hire claims such as this, the courts emphasise the need for careful and proper control of the claims by the application of the doctrine of mitigation".[87]

The Court continued that there was no necessary inconsistency in the decision: "it does not, however, follow that because a person is not able to pay a conventional hire rate for similar cars to be used as minicabs for an open ended period that it was unreasonable for him to fund a total cost of some £3,200 for the repair of the car."[88]

The Court of Appeal accepted that the Judge was entitled to find that – considering all of the evidence before her – over an eight month period, the Claimant could have saved enough to pay for the repairs.[89]

It is also interesting that the Court of Appeal made the obvious point in assessing the reasonableness of the Claimant's actions "this was not the case of a person who was being asked to put himself in a debt position where the alternative is not to be in debt, or not to increase his debt. It

---

86 [2013] EWCA Civ 1299.

87 *Opoku*, para. 13(2).

88 *Ibid.*, para. 23.

89 *Ibid.*, paras 28-30.

is a balance between the debt of £5,000 a month [the credit hire charges] and the alternative of funding £3,400 on a one off basis to repair the car".[90]

Defendants may rely on this case to argue, particularly in cases with a very long period of hire, that the reasonable course of action for a Claimant is to save money over time to pay for repairs or a replacement vehicle. Claimants may take some comfort from the fact that a considerable period of hire was still allowed on the facts of *Opoku*.

At the end of these recent authorities, it is worth highlighting that much still depends on the specific facts of the case. Defendants should seek to establish the cost of repairing / replacing the Claimant's vehicle and whether the Claimant had that money readily available or could have saved it. Claimants might explore why there was a delay in receiving money from the Insurer and whether the Insurer's position was clearly communicated; it is hardly attractive for the Insurer to argue that the Claimant has acted unreasonably when the delay is entirely of their own making.

As a practical point, it is often unattractive for Defendants simply to suggest that something unreasonable must have happened because the hire charges exceed the pre-accident value; there is no golden ratio at which the hire charges become unreasonable. It is more attractive for Defendants to try to identify a moment at which it became unreasonable for the Claimant to continue hiring. For example, it might be argued that once the Claimant received a letter from the Defendant denying liability, he must have realised that the Defendant would not be sending the cheque for pre-accident value any time soon and hence should have reconsidered the hire at that point.

5. Self-Employed Claimants and Businesses

A separate issue of reasonableness can arise in relation to self-employed Claimants who use their vehicle for their business. Suppose that the Claimant's business makes a profit of £1,000 per month. Suppose

---

90 *Ibid.*, para. 31.

further that the Claimant hires a replacement vehicle for work purposes at a cost of £2,000 per month. If the Claimant were to pay the hire charges himself, that would mean that his business would be running at a loss of £1,000 per month. Defendants may argue that this is simply not reasonable; it is certainly "uneconomic". As the disparity in the figures grows, the Defendants argument becomes stronger.

This led one distinguished text book to conclude that in relation to a profit earning chattel *"if, for example, the cost of hiring exceeds the profit which could have been earned, only the latter may be recovered".*[91]

Defendants may rely on this to argue that wherever the loss of profit is lower than the hire charges, only loss of profit should be recovered. Defendants have had some success in this argument in credit hire cases (at least at first instance). Thus in *Singh v Aqua Descaling Ltd,*[92] the court held that *"It is obvious, and I so find, that the cost of hiring exceeded by far the profit which could have been earned; consequently, only the loss of profit can be recovered... and then only for that period reasonably required to achieve a replacement and 'restore' the profit. <u>In this case I am prepared to award six week's loss of net profit</u>"*

Other cases which reached the same result include *A Line Taxis v Ward*[93] and *Ali v Spirit Motor Transport Ltd*[94] (however the latter decision was appealed by the Claimant and compromised by the Defendant before the appeal was heard).

Care is needed before drawing automatic conclusions from these cases. In the first place, it is necessary to be specific about the relationship between the Claimant's business and the vehicle. In relation to private hire vehicles, a different rule may apply to Claimant who own / operate large taxi companies (like the Claimants in *Aqua Descaling v Singh* and *A Line Taxis*) compared to taxi owner / drivers who may have more scope to recover hire charges. In *Aqua Descaling*, the Court indicated that if

---

91 Clark and Lindsell on Torts 20th edition 28-126.

92 Unreported, HHJ Oliver Jones QC, 18 February 2008 at paragraph 9.2.

93 Unreported, Chesterfield County Court, Wall DJ, 2 May 2014.

94 Unreported, Leeds County Court, HHJ Saffman, 24 January 2014.

the Claimant used the vehicle for "private / family purposes" as well as business then hire charges are likely to be recoverable.[95] In *Ali v Spirit Motor Transport Ltd*, the Court tried to resolve this point by awarding loss of profit plus general damages of £15 per day for personal loss of use, but it is open to serious argument whether this mix and match approach is really sustainable.[96]

In any event, even in relation to companies, there is ample scope to argue that the company should not be restricted to loss of profit on the facts of individual cases. First, Claimants may respond that the Defendant is effectively saying that it was unreasonable for him to carry on working following the accident. This comes back to the fundamental question how far a Claimant is expected to go to mitigate his loss. Is the Claimant required to give up his work for the Defendant's benefit?

Second, on appropriate evidence, the Claimant may argue that if they did not have a vehicle they would suffer a loss of goodwill (perhaps even of crucial contracts) which would be more damaging than simple loss of profits. McGregor notes that "a claimant need not prejudice his commercial reputation".[97] If a small business would be unable to service its clients without a vehicle, it may be difficult for a Defendant to show that hiring a vehicle was unreasonable.

Third, Claimants may note that "a claimant need not act so as to injure innocent persons".[98] Thus where the Claimant is a company providing taxis for sub-contracted drivers to use, it is arguable that it is reasonable for it to hire a replacement vehicle because the alternative is effectively to put the innocent driver out of work.

None of these issues appear to have been addressed in the higher courts (as set out above, the Appeal in *Ali v Spirit Motor Transport Ltd* which might have addressed these issues was compromised). The present position is therefore that the question of reasonableness remains one for the

---

95 *Aqua Descaling v Singh*, paragraph 9.3.

96 *Ali v Spirit Motor Transport Ltd*, para. 22.

97 McGregor on damages 7-087.

98 McGregor on Damages 7-086.

courts to decide on the facts of individual cases without specific guidance from higher courts.

CHAPTER FOUR
INTRODUCTION TO
ENFORCEABILITY

A. INTRODUCTION

The next chapters are devoted to the vexed question of whether a particular credit hire agreement is enforceable in the light of various statutory and common law issues, which in particular dictate the form of consumer credit agreements.

The reader should be aware that these issues have a natural life cycle. First, perhaps prompted by new legislation, one insurer begins to argue that particular hire agreements are unenforceable in a few cases. Before long the issue becomes widely known and is litigated, initially at least, in a significant number of low value cases in the County Courts (characteristically with mixed results). Finally, a test case is selected and pursued through the higher courts. Whilst this process is ongoing, the hire companies will, if necessary, amend their agreements and procedures so as to seek to comply with the legislation. Once all the hire companies have successfully amended their agreements or all challenges to enforceability have been rejected by the Courts, the issue will cease to be argued.

As we write, many of the issues based on consumer protection legislation are at the end of this life cycle. Thus after a short period of great activity, arguments based on the Cancellation of Contracts made in a Consumer's Home or Workplace Regulations 2008 ("the Cancellation Regulations") are fading away and the Regulations themselves have been replaced. Moreover, it is rare - though not completely unknown -

for contemporary contracts to fall foul of the 1974 Consumer Credit Act.

Nevertheless, a practitioner cannot afford to be unaware of the issues which arise in these cases. First, small or new hire companies may still have agreements which do not comply with all the relevant legislation. Second, the area of consumer credit or consumer protection is particularly prone to new legislation and new statutory instruments. There were at least 14 new statutory instruments affecting consumer credit agreements in 2010 alone. When novel issues arise under new legislation, the Courts are likely to be guided by the approach taken by the higher courts in respect of earlier legislation. Thus in relation to the 2008 Cancellation Regulations, many of the arguments drew inspiration from the earlier disputes about the Consumer Credit Act. As a result, understanding these principles will help to understand any new enforceability issues which may arise in the future.

The following chapters are designed to help the practitioner to address existing enforceability issues, and also to provide a framework which might be applied to analysing any new enforceability issues in the future.

We will therefore address:-

a) Does enforceability of the credit hire agreement matter? (Chapter Four)

b) Enforceability Issues under the Consumer Credit Acts (Chapter Five)

c) Enforceability Issues under the Cancellation Regulations 2008 (Chapter 6)

d) Other Enforceability Issues (Chapter 7)

Does Enforceability of the Credit Hire Agreement Matter?

Before considering the intricate issues that can arise from considering whether a particular agreement is enforceable, it is worth pausing to ask a logically prior question: <u>why does it matter that the hire agreement is technically unenforceable?</u>

The discussion that follows is informed by the common facts which arise in all these cases. The Claimant enters into a credit hire agreement, as a result of which the Claimant is provided with a replacement vehicle for a number of days. The agreement turns out to be technically unenforceable. The Defendant Insurer raises the unenforceability of the agreement as a defence to a claim by the Claimant for the hire charges.

Claimants may argue that, regardless of enforceability, the Claimant's car was still damaged in an accident that was the Defendant's fault. He still lost the use of his vehicle. The Claimant still needed and, in fact, obtained a replacement vehicle. The individual Claimant, usually, does not wish to challenge enforceability themselves.[1] Why in these circumstances should the Defendant Insurer take the benefit of legislation which was only intended to protect the Claimant? Why can the Claimant not simply claim general damages for loss of use, even where a particular agreement is not enforceable?

We will look first at the resolution of this issue in *Dimond v Lovell*. Second, at the attempts by the hire companies to avoid the result in *Dimond v Lovell* through offering undertakings or subrogation. Third, at whether human rights arguments may assist the hire companies.

B. THE DECISION IN DIMOND V LOVELL

The Claimant in *Dimond v Lovell* argued that it did not matter whether the credit hire agreement between the Claimant and the hire company was unenforceable. It was argued that (a) if the agreement was unen-

---

1 It is usually not advisable for the Claimant to challenge enforceability, since the hire agreement usually contains a clause requiring the Claimant to cooperate with the hire company in pursuing the claim against the Defendant.

forceable, the claimant would be unjustly enriched and (b) that the enforceability of the hire agreement was *res inter alios acta* (literally thing done between / among others). We will deal with these arguments in turn.

a. Unjust enrichment

The Claimant's first argument was that if the hire agreement was unen-forceable then Mrs Dimond would have had the benefit of a replacement vehicle at no cost to herself. She would therefore have been unjustly enriched at the hire company's expense.

Lord Hoffmann addressed this point robustly:

> *"The real difficulty, as it seems to me, is that to treat Mrs. Dimond as having been unjustly enriched would be inconsistent with the purpose of section 61(1). Parliament intended that if a consumer credit agreement was improperly executed, then subject to the enforcement powers of the court, the debtor should not have to pay. This meant that Parliament contemplated that he might be enriched and I do not see how it is open to the court to say that this consequence is unjust and should be reversed by a remedy at common law: compare Orakpo v. Manson Investments Ltd. [1978] A.C. 95."*[2]

Lord Hobhouse also rejected the Claimant's argument:

> *"Again I agree with your Lordships that there is no basis for implying an obligation of the hirer to pay contrary to the statute. Nor is there any basis for the application of some restitutionary principle. The contemplation of the parties was that the hirer should not in fact pay out of her own pocket for the hiring of the car. In the present case she has not been unjustly enriched; her position is precisely that which was intended."*[3]

---

2 *Dimond*, at p 398.

3 *Dimond*, at p405 – 406.

Thus the House of Lords relied on the terms of the relevant legislation to reject the unjust enrichment argument. By enacting the legislation, Parliament had decided that, in order to protect consumers, in certain circumstances an agreement could not be enforced. The Court could not subvert this intention by allowing the hire company to enforce the agreement through the back door by a claim in restitution.

b. Res inter alios acta

The second line of the Claimant's argument was to assert that it did not matter to the success of her claim against the Defendant whether she was liable to pay for the hire.

After reviewing the authorities, Lord Hoffmann stated that:

> "*since high water the tide has retreated. The courts have realised that a general principle of res inter alios acta which assumes that damages will be paid by "the wrongdoer" out of his own pocket is not in accordance with reality. The truth is that virtually all compensation is paid directly out of public or insurance funds and that through these channels the burden of compensation is spread across the whole community through an intricate series of economic links. Often, therefore, the sources of "third party benefits" will not in reality be third parties at all. Their cost will also be borne by the community through taxation or increased prices for goods and services.*"[4]

He then quoted Lord Bridge in *Hunt v Severs*,[5] as Scott V-C had done in the Court of Appeal, and also referred to the fact that for voluntary carers the Claimant "can sue only if he claims as trustee for the person who provided the services". He then concluded:

> "*This case is of course far away from the gratuitous provision of services (usually by a relative) which was considered suitable for recovery as trustee in Hunt v. Severs [1994] 2 A.C. 350. If Mrs.*

---

4 *Dimond*, p399.

5 [1994] 2 AC 350.

Dimond is allowed to sue Mr. Lovell as trustee for 1st Automotive, the effect will be to confer legal rights upon 1st Automotive by virtue of an agreement which the Act of 1974 has declared to be unenforceable. This would be contrary to the intention of the Act. The only way, therefore, in which Mrs. Dimond could recover damages for the notional cost of hiring a car which she has actually had for free is if your Lordships were willing to create another exception to the rule against double recovery. I can see no basis for doing so. The policy of the Act of 1974 is to penalise 1st Automotive for not entering into a properly executed agreement. A consequence is often to confer a benefit upon the debtor, but that is a consequence rather than the primary purpose. There is no reason of policy why the law should insist that Mrs. Dimond should be able to retain that benefit and make a double recovery rather than that it should reduce the liability of Mr. Lovell's insurers."[6] (emphasis added)

Lord Hobhouse made a careful analysis of the basis for loss of use claims and in particular for the claim for hire and stated that whilst "Each case depends upon its own facts", "loss of use of the chattel in question is, in principle, a loss for which compensation should be paid". However, he went on:

"one of the relevant principles is that compensation is not paid for an avoided loss. So, if the plaintiff has been able to avoid suffering a particular head of loss by a process which is not too remote (as is insurance), the plaintiff will not be entitled to recover in respect of that avoided loss."[7]

It should be noted that the approaches of Lords Hoffmann and Hobhouse are not identical. Lord Hoffmann laid emphasis on the breach of the relevant legislation. In similar terms to his rejection of the unjust enrichment argument, he concluded that where a statute has rendered an agreement unenforceable the common law should not step in and render it enforceable again. But he also relied on the risk of double

---

6 *Dimond*, p400.

7 *Dimond*, p406

recovery – if the damages were awarded to the Claimant, she could not be compelled to pay the hire charges to the hire company and so she would recover for her loss twice. Lord Hobhouse's approach was broader and simply emphasised the principle of compensatory loss coupled with remoteness. This distinction has some practical significance, since Claimants may argue that Lord Hoffmann's approach only applies to agreements which are rendered unenforceable by reason of breach of an absolute provision of consumer protection legislation and is tied to situations where there is a risk of double recovery. It would not necessarily apply to common law enforceability arguments for example. Defendants may, however, rely on the broader approach taken by Lord Hobhouse.

The result of *Dimond* was thus that the unenforceability of the hire agreement did bar the Claimant from recovering hire charges.

C. ATTEMPTS TO AVOID THE RULE IN DIMOND V LOVELL

Since the decision in *Dimond*, Claimants have tried various different approaches in order to avoid the conclusion that hire charges are not recoverable.

The Claimant in *Burdis v Livsey* offered an undertaking that they would pay over to the hire company whatever was recovered in damages. This was an attempt to remove the risk of double recovery.

The Court of Appeal was unimpressed:

> *"We think the short answer to these submissions is that double recovery is a bar to the analysis and it is not overcome by the undertaking. Even though the contractual obligations of the claimant to pay Helphire for hire and repairs subsist if the credit agreements are unenforceable Helphire have no enforceable right to recover these amounts. The claimant has not paid and cannot be required to pay them so that if he recovers from the defendant there will be double recovery. The undertaking given to the court is truly collateral and*

*could not be said to be the consequence of the defendant's tort. It is
to be noted that the Court of Appeal was not tempted by a similar
undertaking offered in Dimond"*[8]

In *Bee v Jenson*, the Defendant took issue with the fact that the hire
charges had been paid direct by the Claimant's insurer and were not a
liability owed by the Claimant himself. The Court of Appeal held that
*"it does not follow from the fact that Mr Bee was not liable for the hire
charges of the replacement car that he cannot recover damages for the
deprivation of his use of his car...in so doing he may in legal jargon be
recovering general damages rather than special damages, but there is no significance in that"*[9]

This dicta has been relied on by Claimants to argue that hire charges
may still be recoverable by way of general damages, even in the face of
an unenforceable agreement. At least in the case of consumer protection
legislation where unenforceability is absolute, this reliance appears misplaced because it would run contrary to the House of Lords decision in
Dimond itself.

In *Chen Wei v Cambridge Power and Light Ltd*, the Court resolved the
conflict between the two decisions in this way: *"there is, however, a
material difference between recovering general damages for an admitted
injury and recovering special damages in respect of an alleged debt that is
positively unenforceable under recent policy-based legislation".*[10] In that
case the Court found that, following *Dimond*, no general or special
damages were recoverable.[11] The Court of Appeal reached the same
result in *Salat v Barutis*.[12]

In *Wei*, the Claimant tried to find a further way around *Dimond* by
arguing that the court should not make findings about the agreement,

8 *Burdis v Livsey*, paragraph 58.

9 [2007] EWCA Civ 923, at para 15.

10 Unreported. HHJ Moloney QC, 10 September 2010, para 21a.

11 *Ibid.*, para 25 – 26.

12 *Salat v Barutis* (full reference below), para. 23.

because one party to the agreement (the hire company) was not a party to the action. This too was rejected, with the Court holding that *"provided an issue involving a third party contract is relevant in the RTA case...there is no reason in principle why the fact that the credit hire company is not actually a party should debar the RTA court from dealing with the issue and making findings...A related point, which I do consider valid, is that the RTA court should exercise a proper caution about making such contractual findings"*.[13]

In relation to the 2008 Cancellation Regulations, Claimants have also sought to argue that they had 'affirmed' the contract by bringing the proceedings. The foundation for that argument is a statement by the Advocate General in the European case of *Martin v EDP Editores* that it is for the consumer to decide whether to maintain a contract which was apparently unenforceable.[14] However, in *Salat v Barutis* the Court of Appeal confirmed that *"Whether the Regulations, properly understood, allow a consumer to affirm a contract that would otherwise be unenforceable against him so as to render it enforceable depends on the intention of the legislation."*[15] The Court was inclined to find that the Regulations did not permit affirmation, but did not need to decide the issue because "in order for any affirmation to occur it would be necessary at least for the consumer to know that the contract was unenforceable and, in that knowledge, to express in unequivocal terms his willingness to be bound".[16] On the facts, the Claimant could not establish the factual basis for an affirmation, because there was no evidence that he took any positive action after becoming aware that the agreement was not enforceable.

We should also draw attention to one other possible attempt to distinguish *Dimond*. In *McGuffick v Royal Bank of Scotland*,[17] the High Court accepted that a creditor could continue to report the debtor's out-

---

13 *Ibid.*, para. 2.

14 *Martin v EDP Editores SL*, [2009] ECR 1-11939.

15 *Salat v Barutis*, [2013] EWCA Civ 1499, para. 22.

16 *Ibid.*

17 [2010] 1 All ER 634.

standing amount to credit reference agencies, even though the loan agreement was unenforceable pursuant to the Consumer Credit Act (at least in circumstances where the unenforceability of the agreement could be remedied by the creditor). That reasoning was recently approved and extended to cover irredeemably unenforceable agreements by the Court of Appeal in *Grace v Black Horse Ltd*.[18] This may allow Claimants to argue that even though an agreement is unenforceable, if they do not pay the hire charges they may still be exposed to adverse consequences which were not known at the time of *Dimond*. Claimants may potentially argue that they should not be exposed to the risk of these consequences, at the instance of the tortfeasor. This argument has yet to be ruled on.

D. SUBROGATION / ALREADY PAID

In more recent cases, the Claimant finessed their argument further. Instead of simply relying on an undertaking to pay the charges, which as we have seen failed in *Burdis v Livsey*, Claimants began to arrange for the hire charges to be paid by an insurance company and to argue that, having already been paid, no enforceability issue could arise.

In *W v Veolia Environmental Services (UK) Plc*,[19] the claimant argued that regardless of the enforceability of the agreement, the hire charges had in fact been paid out by an insurance policy. The Claimant argued that the fact that the hire charges had already been paid meant that there was no possibility of double recovery and hence the rationale for disallowing the claim for hire charges in *Dimond* should not apply.

In that case, at the same time as signing the hire agreements, the Claimant had signed a separate agreement to take out an insurance policy in respect of the hire charges. When the Defendant argued that the hire agreement was unenforceable, in what was freely admitted to be a *"litigation tactic"*, the hire company arranged for the insurer to pay the hire charges and to bring a subrogated claim for the loss.

---

18 *Grace and other v Black Horse Ltd*, [2014] EWCA civ 1413, para. 33.

19 [2011] EWHC 2020, HHJ Mackie QC, 27 July 2011.

In spite of the *"informality"* of the insurance arrangements, HHJ Mackie QC sitting in the Mercantile division of the High Court, accepted that there was a valid insurance policy in place and that it had indeed paid out on the claim.[20] This is a vital step in the Claimant's argument – in order to succeed on similar arguments in the future, Claimants would need to provide at least the policy documentation provided in *W v Veolia*.

The Court accepted that the rationale of the decision in *Dimond* was to avoid the prospect of double recovery and consequently held that:-

> *"where a claimant has already paid the hire charges there is no risk of double recovery. The risk of a windfall to a claimant who obtains payment from the defendant but then declines to pay the hire car provider on legal grounds falls away..."[21]*

The Court therefore concluded that the Claimant could recover the hire charges, subject only to the question of whether it was reasonable for the insurer to have paid them. But this mitigation argument proved unsuccessful for the Defendant:-

> *"a claimant who pays a charge for goods or services which he has enjoyed is not failing to mitigate even if it is likely or even probable that he will not have to pay if he takes the matter to court."[22]*

The result was that through the subrogated claim, the Claimant was able to recover damages for the hire charges, even though the hire agreement was unenforceable.

It is perhaps unfortunate that this first instance decision (which as a High Court decision binds County Courts) was not appealed. It would

---

20 *Ibid.*, para. 22.

21 *Ibid.*, para. 37.

22 *Ibid.*, para. 39. The cases referred to in support of this proposition are King v Victoria Insurance Co [1896] AC 250; London v Scottish Building Society v Stone [1983] 1 WLR 1242 and Forde v Birmingham CC [2009] 1 WLR 2732

have been interesting to see how the Court of Appeal addressed the sub-rogation issue.

In particular a number of criticisms might be made of the result:-

> The effect of the decision is that by waving the magic wand of subrogation / payment, the Claimant is possibly able to convert an agreement that Parliament has decided should be unenforceable, into one which can be enforced. Defendants may argue that as a matter of policy this outcome simply cannot be correct. A related point is that it should be possible to tell immediately after the signature of the agreement whether the agreement will be enforceable, rather than it becoming enforceable at a later time;[23]

In *Burdis v Livsey*, the Court of Appeal had considered and rejected the argument that Dr Sen (one of the claimants in that case) could take advantage of payments made by insurers on his behalf. In that case the Court had indicated that recovery would still amount to double recovery.[24] HHJ Mackie was not bound by this conclusion because it was obiter, and held that *"the court does not explain why once payment has been made there would still be double recovery"*. Nevertheless, this suggests at least the possibility that the Court of Appeal might have taken a different view of the matter;

A further peculiarity was that, despite indemnity being limited to £100,000 the insurer in fact paid out £138,000. The Court observed that *"cheerful, prompt and knowing overpayments of claims by insurers is unheard of...I will not treat anything above £100,000 as being a good faith payment of a claim made under the policy."*[25] But this did not affect the result of the case, because on the facts the Court was able to treat the additional £38,000 as arising from a second enforceable contract. It might be argued that these findings about the payment of claim, actually struck at the heart of the insurance arrangements and that the

---

23 This was rejected at para 27 of the judgement in *W v Veolia*.

24 See *Burdis*, para. 56 – 58.

25 *W v Veolia*, para 40.

payment of the additional £38,000 should not have been so lightly severed from the rest of the claim.

Nevertheless, the result of *W v Veolia* is that when faced with any potential enforceability arguments, Claimants may well decide to put in place arrangements for payment through subrogation.

E. HUMAN RIGHTS ISSUES

The effect of the Consumer Credit Act 1974, as originally drafted, was that contracts become automatically unenforceable for relatively minor technical breaches. It has been argued on behalf of the hire companies that this infringes their human rights. Two arguments may arise. First, that rendering an agreement automatically unenforceable deprives the Courts of any discretion and hence remove the hire companies' right to a fair hearing under Article 6 of the European Convention on Human Rights. Second and more promising, that rendering an agreement unenforceable is a disproportionate interference with the hire companies' property rights under Article 1 of the First Protocol to the European Convention.

The human rights arguments were argued before the House of Lords in *Wilson v Secretary of State for Trade and Industry*.[26] Mrs Wilson had pawned her BMW convertible for six months in return for £5,000. She did not repay the loan. Instead she commenced proceedings in the Kingston-upon-Thames County Court arguing that the agreement was unenforceable as it did not comply with the prescribed terms. The pawnbroker relied on the above human rights issues. From modest beginnings, the case snowballed. There were interventions from the Attorney General on behalf of the Secretary of State for Trade and Industry, the Speaker of the House of Commons, four motor insurers and the Finance and Leasing Association.

The House of Lords held that the Human Rights Act 1998 did not apply to Mrs Wilson's contract. The reason was that her cause of action accrued before section 3(1) of the Human Rights Act 1998 came into

---

26 [2003] UKHL 40.

force. This meant that the House of Lords did not need to go on to address the remaining human rights arguments. However, the House of Lords did go on to address them in detail. Whilst their speeches on this issue are strictly obiter, they are likely to be highly persuasive.

Article 6(1)

Article 6(1) guarantees everyone the right to a fair expeditious and public trial of disputes about their civil rights. It includes the implied right of access to the courts. It is not a means of creating new civil rights: it only means that existing civil rights have to be capable of being submitted to a Judge for adjudication.[27]

Lord Nicholls held at paragraph 35 that *"the crucial question...is whether, as a matter of substance, the relevant provision of national law has the effect of preventing an issue which ought to be decided by a court from being so decided".*

He analysed the creditor's complaint as being that: "section 127(3) of the Consumer Credit Act has the effect that a regulated agreement is not enforceable unless a document containing all the prescribed terms is signed by the debtor". In his view this did not engage article 6(1). The reason is that it is:

> *"a restriction on the rights that a creditor acquires under a regulated agreement. It does not bar access to a court to decide whether the case is caught by the restriction. It does bar a court from exercising any discretion over whether to make an enforcement order. But in taking that power away from the court the legislature was not encroaching on territory which ought properly to be the province of the courts in a democratic society."[28]*

The other four members of the House of Lords agreed that article 6(1) was simply not engaged by this case.

---

27 *cf Fayed v UK* (1994) 18 EHRR 393.

28 *Ibid.*, para. 36.

Article 1 of the First Protocol

The issues raised by article 1 of the First Protocol provoked more debate in the House of Lords. It provides:-

> *"every natural and legal person is entitled to the peaceful enjoyment of his possessions. No-one shall be deprived of his possessions except in the public interest and subject to the conditions provided for by law...the preceding provisions shall not, however, in any way impair the right of a State to enforce such laws as it deems necessary to control the use of property in accordance with the general interest."*

The majority of the House of Lords rejected the creditor's arguments for two reasons. First they thought that article 1 of the First Protocol was not engaged. Second they thought if it was engaged, the Consumer Credit Act was proportionate and reasonable.

In relation to whether article 1 was engaged, Lord Hope held at paragraph 109 that article 1 of the First Protocol was not engaged. His reason was that the lender never had an absolute or unqualified right to enforce the agreement or property rights. Article 1 could not be used to confer absolute rights, where they did not previously exist.

Lord Scott at paragraph 168 thought that Article 1 *"is directed to interference with existing possessions or property rights."* Section 127(3) prevented the lender from ever having the right to enforce the agreement. Accordingly article 1 was not engaged.

Lord Nicholls on the other hand thought that article 1 of the First Protocol was engaged. He considered that the effect of the relevant provisions in the Consumer Credit Act was a statutory deprivation of the lender's rights of property rather than a mere delimitation of the extent of those rights. Quite simply, *"the lender's right were extinguished in favour of the borrower by legislation for which the state is responsible".*

It is suggested that Lord Nicholls is correct; there is nothing in the wording of Protocol One to indicate that its protection is limited to absolute or unqualified property rights.

On the second point however all their Lordship agreed: the provisions in the Consumer Credit Act did not violate article 1 Protocol 1.

Lord Nicholls stated at paragraph 68 that inherent in article 1 is the need to hold a fair balance between the public interest and the fundamental rights of creditors. It was common ground that article 1 pursued a legitimate aim: protecting vulnerable persons from exploitation. Therefore the point turned on whether the means employed were proportionate to the legitimate aim.

At paragraphs 74 – 78, Lord Nicholls concluded that the means employed were proportionate. He thought that it was open to Parliament to make compliance with formalities a prerequisite to the enforceability of certain contracts. He noted that *"money lending transactions as a class give rise to significant social problems"*. A uniform solution applied across the board may be the most appropriate was to deal with the problem: a tailor made solution considering the facts of each case may fail to protect the vulnerable. Further, in relation to proportionality, he noted that the Act only applied (at that time) to agreements for less than £25,000. Accordingly he held that section 127(3) was compatible with article 1 of the First Protocol. Lord Hope expressed agreement with Lord Nicholls on this point.

Lord Scott similarly held at paragraph 169 that the provision in the Consumer Credit Act could not be characterised as disproportionate. The reason is that all legal systems have attempted to control money lending transactions. The control measures reflect the vulnerability of those members of the public who need to borrow.

Lord Hobhouse agreed that the Consumer Credit Act did not beyond the measures which are justifiable under that Article.[29] He thought the enforceability provisions a legitimate exercise in consumer protection,

---

29 *Ibid.*, para. 138.

because without effective sanction the rules would be flouted. He too noted the low value of cases to which the Act then applied.

Although the human rights arguments failed in *Wilson*, and there may potentially be less need to resort to them in the future due to the subrogation issue and the reform of unenforceability introduced by the Consumer Credit Act 2006, this does not meant that human rights arguments will always fail in this context. In particular, Claimants may note that the reasons for finding that the measures introduced by s127(3) were proportionate included (1) the perceived social evil of moneylending and (2) the low value of transactions affected.[30] These factors might not apply to other Regulations.

Thus in the cases arising from the Cancellation of Contracts made in a Consumer's Home or Place of Work Regulations 2008, the claimants again sought to argue that the inflexible automatic unenforceability provisions in those Regulations were disproportionate. Here the Claimant's argument was stronger, because the Regulations did not relate to money lending and did relate to transactions of any value. However, here too, the Claimants arguments were rejected. Although in *W v Veolia Environmental Services (UK) Plc*,[31] the point was rendered academic by the Court's decision on subrogation, the Court suggested that the human rights   argument did not assist the Claimant: *"Whatever arguments might be made on a different set of facts I see nothing disproportionate or unlawful in the circumstances of this case, given that the unenforceability would arise only from a failure by Accident Exchange to provide notice to the consumer as clearly required by the Regulations".*[32]

The point was argued more fully in *Salat v Barutis*, but the Court of Appeal held that the case could not properly be distinguished from *Wilson v First County Trust* and therefore there was no violation of Article 1 Protocol 1.[33] It added that the hire company, being presumed

---

30 Note in this regard that when the 2006 Act removed the financial limitation, it removed s127(3) and automatic unenforceability at the same time.

31 [2011] EWHC 2020, HHJ Mackie QC.

32 *Ibid.*, para. 53.

33 *Salat v Barutis*, para. 27.

to understand the Regulations, could have had no expectation of being able to enforce the contract and so no issue of proportionality arose. The Court of Appeal also considered the argument that the Regulations were disproportionate because they contained no exception for small businesses. However, the Court did not need to deal in detail with the argument because the hire company was not a small business - "we are not concerned with cases of the kind to which [the claimant] referred and prefer to express no opinion on them."[34]

It follows that although Claimants have tried to avoid the strict application of *Dimond v Lovell* in a variety of ways, most have failed. Claimants may consider that, in cases where insurance arrangements are in place, arranging for the insurer to pay the hire charges as in *W v Veolia* offers the best chance of recovering the hire charges. As we have seen, other arguments such as affirmation or human rights issues have not been wholly ruled out by the Courts – but thus far no cases have offered a sufficient factual basis for the Courts to distinguish *Dimond*.

---

34 *Ibid.*, para. 28.

CHAPTER FIVE
ENFORCEABILITY ISSUES:
THE CONSUMER CREDIT ACTS

A. Introduction
B. Is a credit hire agreement regulated?
C. What do the Consumer Credit Acts require?
D. What becomes of an Improperly Executed Regulated Agreement?

A. INTRODUCTION

The purpose of this chapter is to discuss the enforceability of credit hire agreements under the Consumer Credit Act 1974 as amended by the Consumer Credit Act 2006. We will deal with the issues in this way:-

1. Is a credit hire agreement regulated by the Consumer Credit Acts?

2. If so, what do the Acts require?

3. What becomes of an improperly executed regulated agreement?

However, we should remind the reader that the heyday of these arguments was in the 1990s. Most credit hire agreements have now been amended so as to avoid the worst effects of the Acts, and the 2006 Act itself draws much of the venom of the earlier statute. As a result the most important issues for practitioners are likely to be (1) the provisions regarding exemptions from the Acts and (2) the effects of unenforceability.

Since many of these issues turn on the interpretation of clauses in credit hire agreements, it is worth beginning with some general observations on contractual interpretation.

Defendants may preface their submissions in this respect by stating that if there is any doubt or ambiguity as to construction, the construction most preferable to the consumer, i.e. the Claimant, rather than the credit hire company should apply. In other words the *contra preferentum* rule should be applied. Thus in *Ketley v Gilbert*[1] Brooke LJ recognised, obiter, that:

> *"if there had been any doubt in the interpretation of the agreement that doubt would have been resolved in favour of [the claimant] as the hirer, so as to render the agreement unenforceable."*

Claimants may counter that contracts should be interpreted as far as possible to give effect to their commercial purpose (in this case to provide the Claimant with a car and for the Claimant to claim back the cost of that car from the tortfeasor). In order to fulfil this commercial purpose the contract would have to be enforceable. Reference may also be made to the rule of construction that it is better for a thing to have effect than to be made void. For example, in *Mills v Dunham*,[2] it was stated:

> *"It is a settled canon of construction that where a clause is ambiguous a construction which will make it valid is to be preferred to one which will make it void."*

B. IS A CREDIT HIRE AGREEMENT REGULATED?

In this section we will consider:

a) Whether the agreement provides credit?

b) The correct classification of credit hire agreements under the 1974 Act

c) Exemptions from the regime of the 1974 act.

---

1 (2001) 1 WLR 986.

2 [1891] 1 Ch 576 at 590.

a) Does the Agreement provide Credit?

In *Dimond v Lovell* in both the Court of Appeal and the House of Lords, the Claimant argued that the credit hire agreement in question did not in fact provide credit.

This apparently unattractive argument was encouraged by the drafting of the Act itself. Section 9 defines "credit" as follows:

> *"(1) In this Act "credit" includes a cash loan, and any other form of financial accommodation."*

This is not necessarily a helpful definition, since it does not state what "credit" means, instead it merely indicates that cash loans and financial accommodation are included within the definition.

Perhaps a more helpful definition of credit is that provided by Professor Goode:-

> *"credit [is] extended whenever the contract provides for the debtor to pay, or gives him the option to pay, later than the time at which payment would otherwise have been earned under the express or implied terms of the contract."*[3]

In *Dimond*, the Claimant argued that the services provided to Mrs. Dimond were not only the use of the car but also the pursuit of her claim. These obligations should be treated as forming part of an entire contract in which 1st Automotive could not recover any part of the consideration until it had not only allowed Mrs. Dimond the use of the car but also brought the claim for damages to a conclusion. Only at this point would 1st Automotive become entitled to payment and therefore the provision for "credit" was not really credit at all. Payment was thus not postponed, they argued, until later than the time at which payment would otherwise have been earned.

---

3   *Goode, Consumer Credit Legislation*, loose leaf ed., vol 1, para. 443.

The House of Lords unanimously held that the agreement provided credit for two reasons. First, the agreement stated on its face that it provided credit. Second, payment was in fact delayed until later than it would otherwise have been earned.

On the first issue, according to Lord Hoffmann the agreement in question provided:-

> "1st Automotive "allow[s] the hirer credit on the hire charges" this arrangement is described as a "credit facility" and if there is a breach of condition 5(iii) the "credit allowed" may be terminated."[4]

The clear and repeated references in the contract to "credit" were according to Lord Hoffmann "unpromising material for an argument".

Lord Hobhouse made a similar point:-

> "Here the terms of the agreement are explicit. The lessor is extending credit to the hirer. It is described as a "credit facility" and the allowance of credit and its termination are specifically referred to. Under these circumstances there can be no escape from the answer which your Lordships have given."[5]

Second, Lord Hoffmann considered that the agreement did allow for the deferral of payment:

> "Th[e claimant's] argument depends upon construing the contract as imposing upon 1st Automotive a duty to Mrs. Dimond to pursue the claim and treating the performance of that duty as forming part of an entire contract which also included the provision of the vehicle."[6]

He went on:

---

4   *Dimond v Lovell*, p394.

5   *Ibid.*, p405.

6   *Ibid.*, p395.

"The only obligation of 1st Automotive under the agreement was to provide the vehicle. In the absence of credit, it would have been entitled to payment during or at the end of the hire. All the provisions about the pursuit of the claim were express or implied conditions that deferred the right to recover the hire and therefore constituted a granting of credit. In addition, of course, the pursuit of the claim by 1st Automotive on behalf of Mrs. Dimond may have given rise to further obligations to her, such as the obligation to indemnify her against a liability for costs which Lord Mustill mentions in Giles v. Thompson [1994] 1 A.C. 142, 163."

By implication, Lords Browne-Wilkinson, Nicholls and Saville agreed with the analysis of Lord Hoffmann on this point.

Lord Hobhouse agreed that on the facts there was a deferral of payment:

"Where the transaction is a relatively simple consumer transaction little sophistication is required. The car has been hired, used and returned. No payment of the hire charges is stipulated for at that time. Payment is postponed until the hirer has been put in funds: "the lessor will allow the hirer credit on the hire charges". But neither the lessor nor the hirer is under an obligation to procure that the hirer is put in funds. The lessor has no obligation; the hirer's obligation is simply to co-operate. As is illustrated by the present case, the accident hire company itself in the contractual document characterised what it was doing as the providing a credit facility. It was clearly right to do so."[7]

However he also expressed doubt about the definition of credit propounded by Professor Goode, and suggested a rather narrower definition.

"The test formulated by Professor Goode adopted by the Vice Chancellor in the Court of Appeal [1999] 3 W.L.R. 561, 572 will not always be a satisfactory one to apply. Many commercial agreements contain provisions which could be said to postpone (or advance) the time at which payment has to be made. Frequently, there will be

---

7   *Ibid.*, p405.

reasons for this other than the provision of credit. Payment may be postponed as security for the performance of some other obligation by the creditor. Payments may be made in advance of performance in order to tie the paying party into the commercial venture. Payment provisions may like any other aspect of the transaction be part of its com mercial structure for the division of risk, for the provision of security or simply the distribution of the commercial interest in the outcome of the transaction."

It therefore seems to be clear that an ordinary credit hire agreement will be understood as providing credit. However Claimants may argue that this result is not inevitable. First, in *Dimond*, one of the terms in the written agreement expressly provided for payment to be deferred and other terms expressly referred to "credit". This made it easy for the House of Lords to decide that credit was provided. Not all credit hire agreements are so transparent. Where an agreement does not include a term deferring payment, it may be more difficult for Defendants to argue that any credit is provided at all. Claimants might argue that the fact that an agreement has not been enforced might be a gratuitous indulgence or a forbearance on the part of the credit hire company and not a contractual deferment of debt. Second, i n *Dimond*, the agreement did not oblige the credit hire company to pursue the Claimant's claim nor suggest that this was part of an "entire agreement". It might remain open to Claimants to argue that there was no deferral of payment, where such terms are included in the contract.

b) The Correct Classification of the Credit Hire Agreements

Sections 8 – 14 of the Consumer Credit Act 1974 go on to divide credit agreements into different categories. It is therefore necessary to consider briefly which categories credit hire agreements fall into.

I n *Dimond*, the categorisation of the agreements was addressed in most detail by the Court of Appeal. Scott V–C concluded:

"In my judgment the 1st Automotive agreement was a personal credit agreement (section 8(1)), a consumer credit agreement (section 8(2)), an agreement for a fixed sum credit facility (section 10(1)(b)), a

restricted-use credit agreement under section 11(1)(a) and a debtor-creditor-supplier agreement under section 12(a)"[8]

In the House of Lords, none of the speeches explicitly analyse exactly what sort of agreement it was. However, Lord Hoffmann referred to paragraph 3(1)(a) of the Consumer Credit (Exempt Agreements) Order 1989 which only applies to fixed sum debtor-credit-supplier agreements. This suggests that he agreed with the Court of Appeal that the agreement was a fixed-sum debtor-creditor-supplier agreement.

Is it also a consumer hire agreement?

An issue which sometimes arises in practice is whether a particular agreement is also a consumer hire agreement as defined by section 15 of the Act. It is advantageous for Defendants to argue that the agreement is a consumer hire agreement because the exemption provisions in paragraph 3(1) of the 1989 Order do not apply to consumer hire agreements.

There appears to be nothing to prevent a particular agreement being both a consumer credit agreement and a consumer hire agreement. The Court of Appeal in *Dimond* concluded that:-

> "[I] am not persuaded that the two regimes would necessarily be incompatible. If certain prescribed requirements have to be included in regulated agreements for the hire of goods and other requirements have to be included in regulated agreements that provide credit, then agreements that both provide for the hire of goods and allow credit for payment of the hire charges may have to include both sets of requirements. If any genuine case of incompatibility were to arise, the Act provides the remedy via an application under section 60(3) for a waiver or variation of the requirements [see below]."[9]

The definition of consumer hire agreement is contained within section 15, which provides:-

---

8   *Dimond v Lovell, CA decision,* para. 69. This was the conclusion of a detailed discussion which extended over paras 27 – 69.

9   *Ibid.,* para. 67.

(1)A consumer hire agreement is an agreement made by a person with an individual (the "hirer") for the bailment . . . of goods to the hirer, being an agreement which –
(a)   is not a hire-purchase agreement and
(b)   is capable of subsisting for more than three months, and
(c)   [...][10]

The critical issue is the meaning of *"capable of subsisting for more than three months"*. Although Defendants have argued that this phrase applies to the duration of the agreement, in *Burdis v Livsey* the Court of Appeal concluded that it applied to the bailment of the car:-

"Although sub-section (1)(b) could have been more clearly drafted we agree with the judge's construction. Section 15 is directed at the long-term bailment of goods which are not the subject of hire purchase agreements. Sub-section (1)(b) is intended to refer to the period of such bailment and not to any other obligations which might be assumed under the agreement. Sub-section (1)(c) is merely intended to limit the application of the section to agreements of a certain size. It does not extend the type of agreement to which the section is intended to refer.

Some support for this construction can be derived from the surrounding sections of the Act. Section 15 appears as one of six sections which closely define different categories of regulated agreements. Section 18 to which we will return contemplates that one must look at any agreement to see whether any part of it falls within one of these defined categories, in which case that part must be treated separately. This suggests that the intention was to confine the different categories of agreement. The construction contended for by

---

10 The 1974 Act included at subsection (c) a clause limiting the definition to agreements where the payments do not exceed £15,000. This financial limitation was removed by the Consumer Credit Act 2006 and no longer applies.

the insurers gives a much wider definition of a consumer hire agreement than we think Parliament intended."[11]

The result is that provided that the hire agreement includes a clause limiting the duration of bailment under the agreement to a period less than three months, the agreement is unlikely to be a consumer hire agreement.

It remains possible for Defendants to argue that the clause limiting the duration of the bailment is a sham, particularly where the hire period in fact lasts more than three months, or multiple hire agreements are signed in respect of the same rental vehicle. But as set out below arguments based on sham are unlikely to succeed in this context. Where the hire period under a single agreement exceeds three months, Claimants may well argue that the contract itself was not capable of subsisting for more than three months, but the Claimant is in breach of a term of that contract.

Section 18: multiple agreements

In *Dimond*, the Claimant also argued in the alternative that the credit hire agreement provided for two things: the provision of a hire vehicle and the provision of credit. It should therefore be treated as a multiple agreement within the meaning of section 18 of the Act. The conclusion that the Claimant hoped to reach was that only the credit part of the agreement would be unenforceable, leaving the hire company able to enforce the hire part of the agreement.

In response to this argument, Lord Hoffmann stated:

> "*The difficulty I have with this argument is that it seems to sever the provisions that create the debt (hiring the car) from the provisions that allow credit for payment of the debt. Whatever a multiple agreement may be, one cannot divide up a contract in that way. The creation of the debt and the terms on which it is payable must form parts of the same agreement. The truth of the matter is that I accept that the hiring agreement was a single contract. But I do not accept Mr. Wingate-Saul's submission as to what that contract was. He argues*

---

11 *Burdis v Livsey*, paras 48 – 49.

that it involved multiple obligations on the part of 1st Automotive that had to be performed over a period starting when the car was hired and ending when the damages were recovered. I consider, on the contrary, that the only primary obligation of 1st Automotive was to provide the car. The rest of the agreement dealt with the conditions upon which it would be entitled to recover the hire. To such an agreement section 18 has, of course, no relevance."[12]

A similar argument was also dismissed by the Court of Appeal in *Burdis*. There, the Claimant argued that the obligation to pay the hire company was free standing from the clauses concerning credit. Therefore, they argued, even if the credit provisions are unenforceable the Claimant will still be obliged to pay the hire company. The Court of Appeal concluded: *"we do not think it is possible to regard these terms as having a free standing life of their own. They are simply part of the terms on which credit is granted."*[13]

Act only applies to Individuals

Both section 8 and section 15 of the Act clearly state that they apply where the debtor or hirer is an "individual". Section 189 of the Act states that "individual" "includes a partnership or other unincorporated body of persons not consisting entirely of bodies corporate". The Act does not therefore protect any form of corporate entity.

Claimants might go further and argue that since the title of the Act only refers to "Consumer", the Act should only apply to consumers, either as defined under European law or perhaps pursuant to the Unfair Contract Terms Act 1977. Therefore, for example, a mini-cab driver who is self-employed and who hires a cab after an accident would not be covered by the Act even though he would come within the definition of individual.

---

12 *Dimond v Lovell*, p396.
13 *Burdis v Livsey*, para. 60.

c) Does the Agreement fall within an Exemption?

Section 16 of the Act empowered the Secretary of State to make Regulations exempting certain types of agreement from the Act (and hence from the rigours of enforceability).

The Consumer Credit (Exempt Agreements) Order 1989 ("the Exemption Order") paragraph 3(1), as amended by Regulation 66 of the Consumer Credit (EU Directive) Regulations 2010 provides:

> *"The Act shall not regulate a consumer credit agreement which is an agreement of one of the following descriptions, that is to say – (a) a debtor-creditor-supplier agreement being either – (i) an agreement for fixed-sum credit under which- (aa) the total number of payments to be made by the debtor does not exceed four, (bb) those payments are required to be made within a period not exceeding 12 months beginning with the date of the agreement and (cc) <u>the credit is provided without interest</u> and without any other charges."* (emphasis added)

The amendment, which entered into force on 1 February 2011, added the requirement at (cc) that in order to qualify for an exemption an agreement must not provide for interest on the credit. The result is that, since most credit hire agreements provide for the payment of interest, they do not fall within the exemption and thus must be treated as regulated agreements.

Much litigation has concerned whether specific agreements comply with what are now conditions (aa) and (bb). We will summarise this litigation below, although it is worth repeating that much of this discussion is now academic since credit hire agreements are likely to fall foul of (cc).

In order to fall within conditions (aa) and (bb) of the exemption, credit hire agreements must satisfy five conditions. The agreement must be:

    i.   for fixed-sum credit,

ii. under which the total number of payments to be made by the debtor does not exceed four and

iii. those payments are required to be made

iv. within a period

v. not exceeding 12 months beginning with the date of the agreement.

i. Fixed-sum credit

Some have attempted to argue that a credit hire agreement does not provide fixed-sum credit within the meaning of section 10 of the Act where there has been no price entered on the agreement.

This argument is misguided. Section 10 defines running account credit as *"a facility under a personal credit agreement whereby the debtor is enabled to receive from time to time (whether in his own person, or by another person) from the creditor or a third party cash, goods and services (or any of them) to an amount or value such that, taking into account payments made by or to the credit of the debtor, the credit limit (if any) is not at any time exceeded"*. It then defines fixed sum credit as *"any other facility"*. Thus under the, admittedly odd, definition in the Act anything which is not running account credit falls within the definition of fixed sum credit.

As Scott V-C approached the question in the Court of Appeal in Dimond: *"It seems clear to me that 1st Automotive's agreement does not allow its customers "running account credit" as described in section 10(1)(a). It follows that... it allows fixed sum credit as described in section 10(1)(b)."*[14]

ii. Four Payments

Defendants may argue that unless the agreement expressly limits the number of payments to four or less it is not exempt.

---

14 *Dimond v Lovell*, CA decision, para. 27.

However, in *Burdis v Livsey*, the Court of Appeal held that:

> *"This issue is simply one of construction of the agreements concerned. Looking at the credit hire agreement the principal obligation is contained in condition 3, the first sentence of which says when the credit period is to expire and continues "at that point you will be liable to pay". This is a one payment requirement."*[15]

Thus where the agreement is silent as to the number of payments, it is likely to be interpreted as a one payment requirement. This result was consistent with the decisions of HHJ Harris in *Seddon v Tekin*[16] and in *Burdis* itself.

iii. Required

If the agreement leaves a discretion as to whether payment will be enforced within twelve months, Defendants may argue that this does not <u>require</u> payment as set down in the Order. Such arguments may be strengthened where payment has not in fact been enforced within that time.

An authoritative analysis of these arguments was carried out in *Seddon v Tekin*, in which HHJ Harris analysed a clause which provided that, "The credit period extended by this agreement shall expire in any event 51 weeks from the date of the agreement. At the expiry of the credit period you shall then become liable to pay the hire charges in full."

He held that this came within the Exemption Order and stated:

> *"In my judgment the hypothetical reasonable person reading the stipulation, "You shall then become liable to pay in full" would understand that to mean that he was required to pay then and not that he may be asked to pay thereafter.*

---

15 *Burdis v Livsey*, para. 52.

16 *Seddon v Tekin and Dowsett v Clifford*, HHJ Harris, Oxford County Court, 25 August 2001.

This approach also accords with the nature of credit. In the Court of Appeal in *Dimond v Lovell*, the Vice Chancellor referred to *Grant v Watton* [1999] STC 330 and cited Pumphrey J where he said: *"Credit is granted when payment is not demanded until the time later than the supply of services or goods to which the payment relates. Credit is the deferring of a payment of a sum which in the absence of an agreement would be immediately payable"*, and said that he entirely agreed with this. Thus at the end of the 51 or 26 weeks credit expires and the charges are immediately due and due without further demand or particularisation. The hirer, if he does not know what they are can always ask.

iv. Within

Defendants may also argue that the wording of the agreement does not fall within the exemption because payment was not required "within" the prescribed twelve months.

This issue came before the Court of Appeal in the case of *Ketley v Gilbert.*[17] The question for the court was whether the clause requiring charges to be paid "on the expiry of 12 months starting with the date of this agreement", satisfied the wording of the 1989 Order. The Court of Appeal held that an agreement permitting the final payment to be made "on expiry" of that period permitted the final payment to be made after the 12-month period had expired. Payment was not required to be made within a period "not exceeding 12 months" which was necessary if exemption was to be afforded to the agreement pursuant to the 1989 Order.

Where payment falls due on the anniversary of the agreement, Defendants may argue that it is not therefore due "within" the twelve months stipulated in the Order.[18]

In other cases, whilst an agreement may make it clear that a credit period comes to an end before the expiration of twelve months, it may also be

---

17 [2001] 1 WLR 986.

18 *cf* further *Zoan v Rouamba* unreported 21/1/2000.

argued that a reasonable time to actually pay the debt would be implied for the Claimant after that date. Thus in *Ketley v Gilbert*, Brooke LJ states:

> *"If the words of the agreement could be flexibly interpreted to permit payment a reasonable time after the expiry of 12 months (since it could not reasonably by expected that the hirer would make payment on the stroke of midnight), such payment was not required to be made within a period not exceeding 12 months, as was necessary if exemption was to be afforded to this agreement pursuant to the 1989 order."[19]*

However, Claimants may argue that if the credit period comes to an end, the clear implication is that payment is then due. Thus in *Burdis v Livsey*, it was argued that once a person becomes liable to pay, he has a reasonable time before he is actually required to pay the money hence taking payment beyond the twelve months. The Court of Appeal rejected this argument: *"liable" may mean "bound or obliged by law" in which sense condition 14 [the relevant provision] would obviously require payment at the end of the credit period or "obliged if asked."[20]*

v. Twelve Months

This is the most technical of all the arguments surrounding the exemption clauses. If an agreement requires payment within twelve months "after" or "from" or "of" the date of the agreement, Defendants may argue that this does not come within the exact wording of the Order since it allows credit for one day more than that permitted by the Order.

In *Zoan v Rouamba*,[21] the Court of Appeal reviewed the authorities on time limits and concluded:

---

19 *Ketley v Gilbert*, para. 26.
20 *Burdis v Livsey*, para. 55 upholding HHJ Harris QC.
21 Unreported, Court of Appeal, 20 January 2000.

"Where, under some legislative provision, an act is required to be done within a fixed period of time "beginning with" or "from" a specified day it is a question of construction whether the specified day itself is to be included in, or excluded from, that period. Where the period within which the act is to be done is expressed to be a number of days, months or years from or after a specified day, the courts have held, consistently since Young v Higgon (1840) 6 M&W 49, that the specified day is excluded from the period; that is to say, that the period commences on the day after the specified day.... Where, however, the period within which the act is to be done is expressed to be a period beginning with a specified day, then it has been held, with equal consistency over the past forty years or thereabouts, that the legislature (or the relevant rule making body, as the case may be) has shown a clear intention that the specified day must be included in the period."[22]

This led the Court of Appeal to uphold the trial Judge's finding that *"it was "obvious", from the use of the expression "beginning with the date of the agreement" in paragraph 3(1)(a)(i) of the 1989 Order, that the period of twelve months prescribed by that paragraph included the date of the agreement."[23]*

The result in that case was the phrase in the contract requiring payment "twelve months after the date of this agreement", permitted payment to be made one day after the twelve month period had expired for the purposes of the Exemption Order. The agreement therefore fell outside the scope of the exemption, and was regulated and ultimately unenforceable.

Is the exemption clause a Sham or Pretence?

Defendant insurers have attempted to argue that the clauses drafted to bring credit hire agreements within the wording of the exemption order are a sham or a pretence.

---

22 *Ibid.*, paras 23 – 24.
23 *Ibid.*, para. 25.

These arguments were rejected by the Court of Appeal in *Burdis v Livsey*. The Court of Appeal adopted the narrow definition of sham propounded by Lord Justice Diplock (as he then was) in Snook v West Riding Investments Ltd:

> *"for acts or documents to be a sham…all the parties thereto must have a common intention that the acts or documents are not to create the legal rights and obligations which they give the appearance of creating".*[24]

The credit hire agreement could not come within this narrow definition of a sham because in credit hire cases there is rarely any evidence of deceit or improper motive on the part of the Claimants. The Court of Appeal were content to quote from the judgment below of Judge Harris QC in the Oxford County Court:

> *"There was no suggestion … that any of the claimants who entered into their credit or insurance agreements had any improper motive whatsoever …. There is no evidence that they had any intention to avoid, legitimately or illegitimately, the application of the consumer credit legislation."*[25]

However the courts remain alert to agreements that are shams in the wider sense that the agreements do not do what they say on the packet. For example in *Antoniades v Villiers*[26] the House of Lords refused to give effect to an agreement which called itself a licence and reserved a right of occupation to the landlord. The reserved right was never intended to be exercised. It was a pretence to avoid the provisions of the Rent Acts.

In *Burdis* the Court of Appeal noted that:

> *"in this type of case the courts have made it clear that they will look at the scheme as a whole if there is more than one transaction and subsequent conduct in order to determine its effect and validity....In*

---

24 [1967] 2 QB 786 at 802.

25 *Burdis v Livsey*, para. 31.

26 [1990] 1 AC 417.

the instant case the court is concerned with consumer protection legislation. It is not possible to contract out of the provisions which regulate some transactions but the Act says that other transactions are exempt. There is therefore nothing wrong with entering or attempting to enter into such a transaction. Either it is exempt or it is regulated and the courts must decide which."[27]

The point was that the court simply had to decide whether the agreement in question meets the requirements of an exempt agreement or not. Guidance was taken from Lord Hoffmann's words in *Norglen Ltd v Reeds Rains Prudential Ltd:[28]*

"The question is simply whether upon its true construction, the statute applies to the transaction. Tax avoidance schemes are perhaps the best example. They either work ... or they do not.... If they do not work, the reason .... is simply that upon the true construction of the statute, the transaction which was designed to avoid the charge to tax actually comes within it. It is not that the statute has a penumbral spirit which strikes down devices or stratagems designed to avoid its terms or exploit its loopholes."

The Court considered that on their face the credit hire agreements were exempt from the Act. The Defendant argued that the court should infer that there was no limit to the credit period because the insurance arrangement was a pretence and was not pursued by the hire company in practice. This failed on the facts. Judge Harris had found as a fact at first instance that there were payments from the insurer to the hire company which had the effect of discharging the Claimants' debts. The source of the insurer's funds was irrelevant. There is nothing unusual about the circular flow of funds around a group of companies. Accordingly the Court of Appeal upheld the Judge's decision that there was no sham or pretence on these facts. For completeness, we quote from paragraphs 39 and 44 of the judgment:

---

27 Burdis v Livsey, paras 32-33.
28 [1999] 2 AC 1.

"These points [relating to the insurance arrangements] were obviously considered by the judge who, as we have said, referred to the scheme as a whole as being sloppily executed and to the insurance arrangement as being artificial. But the documents do show an intention to create genuine insurance arrangements. The underwriting agreement contains many of the terms one would expect to find in such an agreement and there was an assumption of risk by underwriters. Subject to the point about the policy wording, which was obviously a mistake, a claimant would have a valid claim under the policy for the cost of hire and repairs if no payment was made by Angel. In effect the risk assumed by underwriters was of the solvency of the Helphire Group. There is nothing wrong or unusual with insurance arrangements which have this effect...

"We have so far considered the insurers' main attack on the scheme. The fact that customers who did not claim on the insurance were not pursued was not considered in any detail by the Judge. But just because the scheme was, as he said, "sloppily enforced" does not lead to the conclusion that the credit hire and repair agreements were intended to have some meaning contrary to their express terms. Commercial parties may, and often do, choose not to enforce their strict legal rights without intending to create or demonstrate some different state of affairs. Other matters relied on by the insurers about the way in which the Helphire scheme was run do not in our judgment advance their case. Looked at from the claimants' point of view there was no pretence. They got exactly what they bargained for: car repair and hire at little or no cost. It might be said that it is only the insurers' attack on these schemes which has raised the spectre of long term credit because in the ordinary way claims of this kind are settled within weeks of the accident."

In a different context arguments of sham / pretence were also rejected in *Corbett v Gaskin*[29] and *Barker v First West Yorkshire*.[30]

---

29 HHJ Harris QC, unreported, 31 August 2007.

30 Unreported 13 September 2007.

This does not necessarily mean that the issue of pretence / sham is dead. The decision was based on factual findings about how the particular companies and their contracts operated. There may be room for Defendant insurers to argue sham / pretence if on the facts of a different scheme, with a different contractual or corporate set up, no payments are being made by the nominal insurer.

It might also be open to Defendant insurers to argue that the exemption clause is an unfair term within the meaning of the Unfair Terms in Consumer Contracts Regulations 1999.[31]

C. **WHAT DO THE CONSUMER CREDIT ACTS REQUIRE?**

Assuming that the Defendant is able to show that the credit hire agreement is regulated by the Acts, the next question to consider is what exactly the agreement must do in order to comply with the Acts.

Section 60(1) of the Act requires the Secretary of State to "make regulations as to the form and content of documents embodying regulated agreements . . ."

Sub-section (2) says that:

> *Regulations under subsection (1) may in particular:–*
> *(a) require specified information to be included in the prescribed manner in documents, and other specified material to be excluded;*
> *(b) contain requirements to ensure that specified information is clearly brought to the attention of the debtor or hirer, and that one part of a document is not given insufficient or excessive prominence compared with another.*

Section 61 introduces the concept of a regulated agreement being "properly executed". It provides, under sub-section (1), that an agreement is not "properly executed" unless:

---

31 These Regulations are explored in more detail in Chapter 7.

(a) a document in the prescribed form itself containing all the prescribed terms and conforming to regulations under section 60(1) is signed in the prescribed manner both by the debtor or hirer and by or on behalf of the creditor or owner, and

(b) the document embodies all the terms of the agreement, other than implied terms, and

. . . . .

The prescribed terms and prescribed form were set out in the Consumer Credit (Agreements) Regulations 1983 ("the 1983 Regulations").

Paragraph 2 of the 1983 Regulations deals with the form and content of regulated consumer credit agreements and, by sub-paragraph (1), requires them to contain the information set out in column 2 of Schedule 1 of the 1983 Regulations. Where information about financial particulars could not be exactly ascertained, sub-paragraph (2) permitted "estimated information based on such assumptions as the creditor may reasonably make in all the circumstances of the case . . ." to be included.

Paragraph 6(1) of the 1983 Regulations requires that:

"The terms specified in column 2 of Schedule 6 . . . in relation to the type of regulated agreement referred to in column 1 . . . are hereby prescribed for the purposes of section 61(1)(a) . . . and of section 127(3) . . ."

Schedule 6 paragraphs 1 and 5 provide that a debtor-creditor-supplier agreement must contain the following prescribed terms:-

"(a) a term stating the amount of credit; [paragraph 1] and a term stating how the debtor is to discharge his obligations under the agreement to make the repayments, which may be expressed by reference to a combination of any one of the following-
(i) number of repayments;
(ii) amount of repayments;
(iii) frequency and timing of repayments;
(iv) dates of repayment;

> *(v) the manner in which any of the above may be determined; or in any other way, and any power of the creditor to vary what is payable."[Paragraph 5]*

The prescribed term for regulated consumer hire agreements is in paragraph 6 of Schedule 6 and consists of the following:

> *"A term stating how the hirer is to discharge his obligations under the agreement to pay the hire payments, which may be expressed by reference to a combination of any of the following– (a) number of payments; (b) amount of payments; (c) frequency and timing of payments; (d) dates of payments; (e) the manner in which any of the above may be determined; or in any other way, and any power of the owner to vary what is payable."*

A term stating the amount of credit

Whilst the interpretation of many of the prescribed terms is straightforward, some difficulty has arisen over the meaning of "a term stating the amount of credit".

In the Court of Appeal in *Dimond*, the Claimant argued that it would not have been possible to have included the prescribed term. i.e., the amount of credit, since the length of the hire period would not be known. Scott V–C disagreed:

> *"But the daily rate of hire would be known and an estimate of the period of hire could be obtained from the garage that was repairing the damaged vehicle. In these circumstances paragraph 2(2) of the 1983 Regulations would, as I have read it, apply and would have allowed 1ˢᵗ Automotive to insert an estimate of the amount of credit with an indication of the assumptions on which the estimate was made. I do not accept that 1ˢᵗ Automotive could not have complied with the Regulations."*[32]

---

32 *Dimond v Lovell*, CA Decision, para. 71.

This statement remains the best judicial guidance on the point. However, Defendants may argue that it is wrong to suggest that an estimate may be applied to Schedule 6 since paragraph 2(2) of the 1983 Regulations allows estimates to be made only for those particulars set out in paragraphs 9 to 11 of Schedule 1 and not for those required by Schedule 6.

Claimants may potentially argue that entering the price of the hire at the time was enough. If there is a three month clause, they can argue that that is the maximum period of hire and therefore the amount of credit can be worked out.

However, Defendants can argue that Scott V–C's comments suggest that the agreement needs to go further and in fact an estimate of the period of hire also needs to be included. Credit hire companies will therefore be able to argue that they have included the "amount of credit" if they have included the daily rate and the estimated time of hire. Even if such an estimate of the period of hire is included, Defendants will be able to argue that this is inadequate if the estimate does not actually end up being accurate as to the actual period of hire.

It is likely that the prescribed terms must be included in the agreement itself, rather than any collateral agreement in writing or orally. Paragraph 1296 of Consumer Credit, edited by Professor Goode, states:

> "Schedule 6 to the agreements regulations sets out the terms prescribed by s 61(1)(a) of the Act, that is, terms which are required to be contained in the executed agreement itself and not merely in some other document embodied in it by cross-reference."

D. WHAT BECOMES OF AN IMPROPERLY EXECUTED REGULATED AGREEMENT?

The final question that must be addressed is, assuming that the credit hire agreement is a regulated, what is the result of failing to include the prescribed terms or prescribed forms?

Section 65 of the Act provides that:

> *"(1) An improperly-executed regulated agreement is enforceable against the debtor or hirer on an order of the court only."*

At the time when *Dimond* was decided, section 127(3) of the Act required a court to dismiss an application for an enforcement order under section 65(1) *"unless a document (whether or not in the prescribed form and complying with regulations under section 60(1)) itself containing all the prescribed terms of the agreement was signed by the debtor or hirer (whether or not in the prescribed manner)".*

This informed the decision in Dimond that that the hire agreement, not containing the prescribed terms, was automatically unenforceable and hence that the hire charges could not be recovered. It also created what was sometimes analysed as a two tiered system, where failure to comply with the prescribed terms led to automatic unenforceability whereas failure to comply with the prescribed form led to possible unenforceability, subject to an enforcement order from the Court.

However, with effect from 6 April 2007, section 127(3) has been repealed by the Consumer Credit Act 2006.

Now in respect of all improperly executed credit agreements, enforceability is governed by section 127(1) :

> *"the court shall dismiss the application [for an enforcement order] if, but only if, it considers it just to do so having regard to (i) prejudice caused to any person by the contravention in question, and the degree of culpability for it"*

In considering whether to grant the enforcement order the court may "reduce or discharge" any part of the sum payable to compensate for prejudice suffered by the debtor (Section 127(2)). Further the court retains the powers in section 135 and 136 to make the enforcement order conditional, suspend the operation of any term of the order and amend any term of any agreement as a consequence of making the order.

There is little guidance on what principles would be applied with regard to an enforcement order. The notes to the Act provide some help but not with respect to the particular example of credit hire.

The result is clear: an improperly executed regulated agreement is no longer automatically unenforceable. Rather it remains potentially enforceable by order of the Court. The question remains what effect this has on the recoverability of hire charges.

Claimants may argue that they should recover the full amount on the basis that there is a potential liability. A similar argument succeeded in cases including *Hatfield v Hiscock*.[33]

On the other hand, Defendants may argue that the proper approach is for the court to assess the probability of an enforcement order being granted in the future. If the probability of enforcement is less than 50%, then it may be argued that the Claimant has not proved his claim. This approach was adopted in *Aggett v Aston Rothbury Factors Limited*[34] in which the Judge stated (obiter):

> *"the prospect of a court granting the s.65 order would not be high where – as here – the evidence was that the claimant would not have entered into the transaction if he had appreciated that he might have had to pay the full amount of the hire charges in the sums finally claimed by Crash Care, and that he was committing himself to them by signing the hire agreements. Had there been compliance with the provisions of the Statute, then it is likely that this Claimant would not have entered into the agreements. In those circumstances, I find that the chances of a court making a section 65 order low....*

---

33 [1998] CCLR 68; [1998] 6 CL 88. See also *Marchant and Marchant v Brown*, unreported, 2/8/1999 (HHJ Poulton), *Knott v Stott*, unreported, 29/9/1999, *Jones v Lindon*, unreported, 26/7/1999, *Pitt-Miller v Patel*, HHJ Marr-Johnson, Mayor's & City County Court, 24 July 2001 and *Wood v Gell*, HHJ Poulton, Canterbury County Court, 27 July 2001.

34 HHJ Overend, Exeter County Court, 6 July 2001.

It seems to me that on the state of the evidence before the Court the prospects of Crash Care being able to recover the credit hire charges from the claimant are negligible…For those additional reasons, I find for the Defendant in relation to the sole issue before the Court, namely the recoverability of the hire charges."

These issues have not been tested under the Consumer Credit Act 2006. It remains unclear exactly what approach the Court would adopt. The issue is therefore open to be tested in the future.

CHAPTER SIX
CANCELLATION OF CONTRACTS MADE AT A CONSUMER'S HOME OR PLACE OF WORK REGULATIONS 2008

A. Introduction
B. When did the Cancellation Regulations apply
C. Exemptions from the Cancellation Regulations
D. What did the Regulations Require?
E. What are the consequences of failing to comply?

A. <u>INTRODUCTION</u>

The Cancellation of Contracts made in a Consumer's Home or Place of Work Regulations etc 2008 ("the Cancellation Regulations") came into force on 1 October 2008.[1] They gave further effect to the Doorstep Selling Directive,[2] and were enabled by the Consumers, Estate Agents and Redress Act 2007. In short they provided that, where the Regulations apply, the trader must give to the consumer a notice of their right to cancel the agreement. If this cancellation notice is not given, the Regulations provide that the agreement "shall not enforceable against the consumer".[3]

These Regulations provoked a flurry of litigation, particularly in the credit hire context.[4] It transpired that some credit hire companies had not provided a cancellation notice at all, and in other cases Defendants subjected the drafting of the cancellation notice to detailed scrutiny to test whether it complied with the Regulations. We can now stand back and summarise the results of these skirmishes.

---

1 Regulation 1, Cancellation Regulations 2008.
2 Council Directive 85/577/EEC
3 Regulation 7(6).
4 Though of course their application is broader and all tradesmen including plumbers, electricians and others were potentially affected by the Regulations.

However, we should start by acknowledging that the 2008 Cancellation Regulations have now been repealed and replaced by the Consumer Contracts (Information, Cancellation and Additional Charges) Regulations 2013. The 2008 Regulations do not apply to credit hire agreements made after 13 June 2014. The new regulations do provide that the trader must provide the consumer with specified information including about cancellation. But the consequences of failing to comply are largely criminal and there is no automatic unenforceability provision. As a result, the new regulations do not assist Defendants in credit hire cases.

The material in this Chapter thus only directly concerns agreements made on or before 12 June 2014. For later agreements, this chapter is only relevant insofar as it sets out general principles or identifies the general approach to enforceability issues.

For those readers who are most interested in the already paid / subrogation issues or the human rights issues that arose under these Regulations, we refer back to the discussion in Chapter Four.

B. WHEN DID THE CANCELLATION REGULATIONS APPLY?

Regulation 5 provided:-

> *"these Regulations apply to a contract, including a consumer credit agreement, between a consumer and a trader which is for the supply of goods or services to the consumer by a trader and which is made-*
>> *(a) During a visit by the trader to the consumer's home or place of work, or to the home of another individual;*
>> *(b) During an excursion organised by the trader away from his business premises; or*
>> *(c) After an offer made by the consumer during such a visit or excursion."*

A credit hire agreement is plainly a contract for the supply of services by a trader.

The first condition which must be met for the Cancellation Regulations to apply to a particular credit hire agreement is that the Claimant must be a *"consumer"*.

Consumer was defined as *"a natural person who in making a contract to which these Regulations apply is acting for purposes which can be regarded as outside his trade or profession"*.[5]

The reference to a *"natural person"* plainly excludes corporations. However, the issue sometimes arises whether a self-employed taxi driver or an individual who uses their vehicle for the purposes of their profession falls within the definition of a consumer.

Defendants may argue that in applying the Unfair Contract Terms Act 1977,[6] the Courts have held that where a business makes a contract of a kind which is not a regular part of its business, it may act as a consumer.[7] Under this expansive definition, a potentially broad category of individuals would fall within the scope of the Regulations.

However, since the Regulations originate in European legislation, Claimants may respond that it is necessary to look at the narrower definition of *"consumer"* which the European Court of Justice has adopted in similar cases. Thus in *Di Pinto*, concerning the definition of consumer under the doorstep selling directive, the Court observed that the wording of the definition:

---

5 Regulation 2(1).

6 Section 12 by which a person is a consumer if "he neither makes the contract in the course of a business nor holds himself out as doing so".

7 *R & B Custom Brokers Ltd v United Dominions Trust Ltd* [1988] 1 WLR 321, in which the Court of Appeal distinguished between transactions which are "integral parts of the businesses" (not acting as a consumer) and those which are not.

"does not make it possible, with regard to acts performed in the context of such a trade or profession, to draw a distinction between normal acts and those which are exceptional in nature."[8]

In that case, the European Court concluded that acts which are preparatory to the sale of a business fall outside the definition of a consumer. In so doing the Court seemed to limit the definition of a consumer to contracts for *"family or personal requirements"*. In the later case of *Benincasa v Dentalkit Srl*, the Court was even more prescriptive:-

"only contracts concluded for the purpose of satisfying an individual's own needs in terms of private consumption come under the provisions designed to protect the consumer... The specific protection sought to be afforded by those provisions is unwarranted in the case of contracts for the purpose of trade or professional activity."[9]

Further, dealing specifically with contracts with a dual purpose, both business and personal, the European Court has held: *"the benefit of those provisions cannot, as a matter of principle, be relied on by a person who concludes a contract for a purpose which is partly concerned with his trade or profession and is therefore only partly outside it. It would be otherwise only if the link between the contract and the trade or profession of the person concerned was so slight as to be marginal"*[10]

Claimants may rely on these European authorities to argue that wherever a contract is partly connected to an individual's trade or profession, he is not a consumer for the purposes of these Regulations. Defendants may argue that this narrow definition of consumer produces odd results. Would the individual who buys a car for domestic and personal reasons but also sometimes uses the vehicle to commute to work, really not be treated as a consumer?

Assuming that the Claimant was a consumer, the Regulations are triggered primarily if the contract was made during a visit by the trader

---

8 [1991] ECR 1-1189 at 15.

9 [1997] ECR 1-3767 at 17.

10 *Gruber v Bay Wa*, Case C-464/01 at para. 39.

to the consumer's home or place of work. In *Chen Wei v Cambridge Power and Light*, the Court was faced with facts typical of a credit hire case. The Claimant had at least one initial telephone conversation with the hire company. Then the hire vehicle was delivered to his home address, at which point he saw the contractual documents for the first time and signed them.

At first instance it was held that the contract was made when the Claimant signed the agreements and hence the Regulations applied. On appeal, the Claimant sought to argue that the agreement had been made in the course of the earlier telephone call. HHJ Moloney QC rejected this argument for two reasons. First, he held that "*the question whether a contract has been sufficiently agreed in the course of telephone conversations, or whether those discussions were merely preliminaries to the making of a written contract at the consumer's home, is one of mixed fact and law for the trial Judge no sufficient reasons were put before me to overturn the fact elements in that finding.*"[11] Second, the written agreement contained an entire agreement clause which the Court held "*has the effect of revoking any prior oral agreement.*"

This suggests that in contracts containing an entire agreements clause, there is likely to be little scope for dispute; the contract is made when the written agreement is signed. In other cases, it may be open to Claimants to argue that the contract was made during the preceding telephone call, provided that the evidence about that call is sufficiently cogent to demonstrate that a concluded agreement was reached.[12]

In *W v Veolia Environmental Services Ltd*, the Claimant sought to avoid the conclusion that the Regulations applied in similar circumstances, by arguing that the Regulations were never intended to apply to mere delivery of a pre-arranged service. This argument had a strong found-

---

11 Unreported 10 September 2010 at para. 11.

12 It may be worth noting that in practice the claimant may need to rely on more than simply the Claimant's evidence in this regard. Experience shows that individuals are unlikely to recall the detail of the initial telephone call in sufficient detail. Evidence may therefore need to be led of any log / record of the telephone call, or from the hire company itself.

ation in the *travaux preparatoire*[13] and certain principles of statutory interpretation.[14] But these arguments were rejected. The Court concluded, obiter:-

> *Parliament has chosen to make the Regulations pursuant to the relevant European Directive and to do so in a particular way following the lengthy consultations to which [counsel for the claimant] has drawn attention... They are not ambiguous... There is no warrant to give these Regulations a meaning beyond that conveyed naturally by the words used*"[15]

Many of these arguments were dealt with briefly by the Court of Appeal i n *Salat v Barutis*. The Court rejected the submission that the agreement was made in the initial telephone call as being "at odds with both commercial common sense and everyday experience, as well as unsupported on the evidence".[16] The Court rejected the further submission that the word "made" encompasses all the exchanges between the contractual parties, holding that "a contract is made for the purposes of regulation 5 when and where it is concluded".[17]

The underlying reasoning of the Court of Appeal in *Salat* and the High Court in *W v Veolia*, is simply that the wording of the Regulations was unambiguous and did not allow for more than one interpretation. As a result, there was little scope for argument about the construction of the agreements.[18]

---

13 *Cf* the explanatory note to the Consumers Estate Agents and Redress Act 2007, the OFT report Doorstep Selling (May 2004) and Government Papers entitled Doorstep Selling and Cold Calling. Claimants may argue that these are entirely directed at the perceived evil of high pressure doorstep selling

14 *See* Bennion on Statutory Interpretation, in particular that provisions which impose criminal sanctions should not be expansively construed.

15 W v Veolia, para. 51.

16 *Salat v Barutis*, para. 14.

17 Ibid., para. 18.

18 *Ibid.*, para. 19.

Where the agreement is signed at the repairing garage or elsewhere, however, the Regulations appear not to apply. Defendants have sought to argue that where the hire company arranges for the Claimant to collect the vehicle and sign the agreements in a third location, this is an excursion within the meaning of paragraph 5(b). This argument has met little success. There are two obstacles to this line of argument. First, whilst the statute gives no definition of *"excursion"* it is difficult to see that it applies in this context. The Regulations appear to be directed against time share selling. Moreover the natural meaning of excursion implies a pre-arranged journey to a particular location and back, arranged by the trader. However here, the consumer is free to get to the garage any way they choose and to leave in any direction. Second, given the variety of companies involved in credit hire and repair, it may be difficult to show that the excursion was organised by the credit hire organisation itself.[19]

Finally, we should note that the Regulations applied in *Wei* and *W* because the written agreement was passed to the Claimant on delivery and signed by him in the presence of the delivery driver. It would be possible for hire companies (and other traders) to avoid the application of these Regulations by amending their standard procedures so that, for example, the written agreement is sent to Claimants through the post or is executed online.[20]

---

19 These difficulties were fatal to the Defendant's position in *Osmond v Gammon*, HHJ Hughes QC Winchester County Court

20 Of course this would not avoid regulation altogether, it is just that a different set of Regulations would likely apply. For instance the Consumer Protection (Distance Selling) Regulations may well apply. They require the supplier to provide the consumer with certain information prior to and after the conclusion of the contract, and also provide for a cooling-off period within which the contract can be cancelled. But they make no provision for unenforceability. Instead Regulation 26 obliges an enforcement authority to look into complaints.

C. EXEMPTIONS FROM THE CANCELLATION REGULATIONS

Regulation 6 provides that the Regulations do not apply to certain contracts including: *"a cancellable agreement"* and *"a consumer credit agreement which may be cancelled by the consumer in accordance with the terms of the agreement conferring upon him similar rights as if the agreement were a cancellable agreement"*.[21]

A "cancellable agreement" refers to a consumer credit agreement regulated by the Consumer Credit Act 1974 which may be cancelled by the debtor or hirer by virtue of Section 67 of that Act.[22]

To summarise the relevant provisions of the 1974 Act, section 67 provides that a *regulated agreement may be cancelled by the debtor or hirer in accordance with this Part"*. In the case of such agreements, section 64 provides that the creditor must give the debtor a notice of cancellation rights, in the prescribed form, indicating how and when the right to cancel is exercisable. In default, a cancellable agreement is not properly executed and hence may not be enforced without an order of the Court.[23] Section 68 allows the debtor to cancel the agreement primarily by the end of the fifth day following the day on which he was notified of the cancellation right.[24]

In order to show that a particular hire agreement was exempt from the Cancellation Regulations therefore, the claimant would need to show either (1) that the agreement was a cancellable agreement or (2) that the cancellation rights specified in the contract are similar to those in a cancellable agreement.

---

21 Regulation 6(1)(b) and (c).
22 Regulation 2(1) provides that "cancellable agreement has the same meaning as in section 189(1) of the 1974 Act. Section 189(1) in turn defines cancellable agreement by reference to s67.
23 See section 65(1) in particular.
24 See section 68(a) and note that a longer period of fourteen days applies in certain circumstances.

In relation to the first possibility, there are likely to be two difficulties for the claimant in arguing that the hire agreement is a cancellable agreement. First, in order to argue that the agreement is a cancellable agreement, the claimant would need to show that it is a regulated agreement (ie not an exempt agreement). This is problematic because many hire agreements specify that they are not intended to be regulated agreements and because in principle many hire companies may be reluctant to argue that their agreements are regulated, as this may expose them to enforceability issues. Second, the cancellation requirements under the Act are hardly any less stringent than under the Regulations, so there is little advantage in advocating that one applies over the other.

However, where a hire agreement contains a cancellation notice which does not quite meet the requirements of the 2008 Regulations (hence would be unenforceable if the Regulations applied), it might be open to the claimant to argue that the cancellation rights that he was provided with were similar rights to those required of a cancellable agreement.

Of course it is unlikely to be enough for claimants to simply assert that the rights provided were similar. Rather the claimant would need to forensically analyse the rights accorded to consumers in the case of cancellable agreements, and compare them to the rights he was given. In the main this would seem to require a cooling off period of five days, and also the rule that where the agreement is cancelled the debtor ceases to be liable to pay any money.[25] However, the exemption only requires the rights to be "similar" and not "identical". This allows the claimant to argue that so long as some form of cancellation notice has been provided which does not obviously disadvantage the consumer, the strictures of the Regulations can be avoided. This argument has not been tested in the higher courts.

---

25 Section 70(1)(b).

D. WHAT DID THE REGULATIONS REQUIRE?

Where the Regulations apply, the consumer has the right to cancel the contract within the cancellation period.[26] The cancellation period is defined by Regulation 2(1) as a period of seven days starting with the date of receipt of a cancellation notice.

Moreover, the trader is required to give to the consumer a notice explaining the consumer's right to cancel the contract.[27]

The Regulations prescribe the form and content of the cancellation notice. These requirements include that the notice must be dated, it must indicate the consumer's right to cancel the contract and it must contain both the information set out in Schedule 4 to the Regulations and a detachable slip for the consumer to return, in the form set out also in Schedule 4.[28] If the trader elects to incorporate the notice into the agreement, it must *"be set out in a separate box"* with a prescribed heading.[29]

Furthermore, Regulation 7(4) provides that where the contract is in writing, the cancellation notice must be *"incorporated in the same document"*. In a number of cases, the Defendant argued that where the cancellation notice was provided on a separate sheet of paper it was not incorporated in the same document.[30]

Resolution of this issue is likely to depend on a careful analysis of the contractual documentation in question. The cases indicate that the fol-

---

26 Regulation 7(1).

27 Regulation 7(2).

28 Regulation 7(3).

29 Regulation 7(5).

30 The Claimant succeeded in *Lawford v Pacey*, HHJ Coltart, 26 August 2010, *Orley v Viewpoint Housing*, HHJ Armstrong 7 December 2010, *Fay x AXA* HHJ Walton 25 February 2011, *Larcombe v Arnold Clark* HHJ Cotter QC, 28 February 2011 and *Trimble v AXA* HHJ Harris QC 12 May 2011 ; but the Defendant was successful in Guerrero v Nykoo HHJ Vosper QC 25 October 2010 and *Rennie v Vasey* HHJ Taylor 7 February 2011.

lowing points are likely to be relevant: whether the notice and the agreement were given to the consumer at the same time; whether the notice refers to the agreement; whether the agreement refers to the notice; whether they bear the same reference number.

E. **WHAT ARE THE CONSEQUENCES OF FAILING TO COMPLY?**

Regulation 7(6) provides that:

> "*a contract to which these Regulations apply shall not be enforceable against the consumer unless the trader has given the consumer a notice of the right to cancel and the information required in accordance with this Regulation*"

This appears to mean that where no cancellation notice is provided, the agreement becomes automatically and irredeemably unenforceable.

In order to avoid this stark conclusion, the Claimant in *Wei* argued that by accepting the hire vehicle and brining a claim to recover the hire charges, he had affirmed the contract. He argued that the wording of Regulation 7(6) deliberately preserved the possibility of a consumer deciding not to cancel the agreement. He relied in this regard on *Martin v EDP Editores*[31] in which paragraph 76 of the Advocate General's opinion indicates *"he [the consumer] must also have the possibility of deciding for himself whether or not he will maintain in force the contract"*. The Claimant argued that this suggested that it was possible for a contract to be maintained under the relevant EU Directive even though there was no cancellation notice.

HHJ Moloney QC rejected this submission. He concluded that based on the drafting of the 2008 Regulations if the Claimant did not seek to take a point on the Regulations, it would be the court's duty to take the point itself. Further he held that it is not open to the Claimant to argue that he affirmed the contract by any conduct prior to the time when he

---

31 (2010) 2 CMLR 27.

was actually informed of his right to cancel.[32] In *W*, the Court indicated that it would have rejected the Claimant's position for the same reasons given by HHJ Moloney QC.[33] The Claimant also failed on these issues in *Salat v Barutis* at Court of Appeal level.

Where a cancellation notice is provided, but it does not comply with the prescribed language of Regulation 7 or Schedule 4, it would appear that the contract is also unenforceable. However Claimants might argue that on a literal reading, provided that a cancellation notice has been provided which includes *"the information required"* (but does not comply with all the formalities) Regulation 7(6) would not be triggered.

Further in such circumstances there might be scope for the Claimant to argue that the hire company had substantially complied with the Regulations and hence the sanction of unenforceability ought not to be required. However Defendants may respond that the Cancellation Regulations themselves provide that contracts are either enforceable or unenforceable. They do not make any provision for partial compliance. In the context of consumer protection, Defendants may argue that this absolute distinction is justified.

---

32 *Chen Wei,* paras 18 and 19.

33 *W v Veolia,* paragraph 38.

CHAPTER SEVEN
OTHER ENFORCEABILITY
ISSUES

In this chapter, we address other issues related to enforceability which may arise in relation to credit hire agreements whether by statute or at common law. These are:-

a) the Consumer Contracts (Information, Cancellation and Additional Charges) Regulations 2013;

b) the concept of Unfair Relationships;

c) the Unfair Terms in Consumer Contracts Regulations 1999;

d) issues arising from signature of the hire agreement;
    i.   no signature;
    ii. late signature;
    iii. agreement not signed by the Claimant;
    iv. bailment;

e) oral assurances / representations;

f) claimant is a minor;

g) illegality.

Defendants should however bear in mind that many of these arguments share a common weakness. As set out in Chapter Four above, it is not enough for the Defendant (who is not a party to the credit hire contract) to identify some legal flaw with the contract. Rather the Defendant needs to show that the agreement is not enforceable against the Claimant. Since many of the above issues would (at best) render the hire agreement voidable at the Claimant's instance, the Defendant is unlikely to be able to show that the agreement is irredeemably unenforceable. Outside the context of consumer protection legislation, arguments founded on restitution are also likely to carry greater weight. The result is that it is more difficult for the Defendant to establish that the hire charges cannot be recovered through these avenues.

A) THE CONSUMER CONTRACTS (INFORMATION, CANCELLATION AND ADDITIONAL CHARGES) REGULATIONS 2013

With effect from 13 June 2014, the Consumer Contracts (Information, Cancellation and Additional Charges) Regulations 2013 replaced the Consumer Protection (Distance Selling) Regulations 2000 and the 2008 Cancellation Regulations.

The new Regulations apply to distance contracts, off-premises contracts and on-premises contracts.[1] Different requirements apply to the different types of contracts, but each require the trader to provide specified information including about the consumer's cancellation rights.[2]

There is currently limited caselaw on the application of the Regulations and none in a credit hire context.

It is worth making two observations. First, the definition of consumer is "an individual acting for purposes which are wholly or mainly outside that individual's trade, business, craft or profession".[3] In some cases, that may give rise to disputes about whether a hire contract is entered into for purposes which are "mainly outside" the individual's trade. It is clear though that corporate claimants are excluded from the definition of consumer. Moreover, private hire vehicle drivers would be unlikely to be regarded as consumers where they hire a vehicle to use for their work.

---

1 Pursuant to the definitions section in Regulation 5, on-premises contracts are the residual category catching all contracts between a consumer and a trader which do not fall into either of the other categories.

2 See Regulations 9-14.

3 Regulation 4.

Second, as mentioned in the previous chapter, the primary sanction for failing to comply with the Regulations, at least as regards notice of the right to cancel, is criminal.[4] Failing to provide the required information is a summary offence, capable of attracting a fine not exceeding level 5 of the standard scale.[5]

B) UNFAIR RELATIONSHIP

Section 140A of the Consumer Credit Act (as amended by the Consumer Credit Act 2006) provides that:

> *"the court may make an order under section 140B in connection with a credit agreement if it determines that the relationship between the creditor and the debtor arising out of the agreement is unfair to the debtor because of one or more of the following:*
>
> (a) *any of the terms of the agreement and any related agreement;*
>
> (b) *the way in which the creditor has exercised or enforced any of his rights under the agreement or any related agreement;*
>
> (c) *any other thing done (or not done) by, or on behalf of, the creditor (either before or after the making of the agreement or any related agreement."*

This section replaced the provisions in the 1974 Act which prohibited "extortionate credit bargains". Although the old provisions were intended to protect consumers, they had limited impact because it was too difficult for consumers to prove that a particular bargain was "extortionate". It might therefore be expected that the new concept of an "unfair relationship" is designed to give the Court greater scope to protect vulnerable consumers.

The first question which must be determined under Section 140A is whether the relationship between creditor and debtor which arises out

---

4   Regulation 19(1).

5   Regulation 19(2).

of the agreement is "unfair". In assessing this, the Court should "have regard to all matters it thinks are relevant" (section 140A(2)).

It remains to be seen what sort of factors will persuade a court that a relationship is unfair. No further guidance is given in the statute. However it is suggested that the courts may draw guidance from the definition of unfair in the Unfair Terms in Consumer Contracts Regulations 1999 (see below).

Interestingly, some further protection is given to the consumer by section 140B(9) which reverses the ordinary burden of proof, so that if a debtor alleges that a relationship is unfair, the burden of proof rests on the creditor to prove that it is not unfair.

Defendants may argue on the right facts that a credit hire agreement gives rise to an unfair relationship. For example it is frequently the case that the Claimant has not read or had explained to them the terms of the agreement that they sign up to. All too often Claimants think that the hire car is free. This might render a relationship unfair.

If an agreement is found to be unfair, then the Court has the discretion to remedy the unfairness by exercising the wide ranging powers set out in section 140B. These include the power to set aside any duties imposed on the debtor by the agreement (section 140B(1)(e)). Effectively this could render the contract unenforceable against the Claimant.

Defendants may argue that section 140A applies to all credit hire agreement, even those which are otherwise exempt from regulation. The basis for this argument is that section 140A applies simply to "credit agreements", whereas other sections in the legislation refer to "regulated agreements". The subtle point is that section 16 divides credit agreements into those which are regulated and those which are exempt. Most credit hire companies have managed to make their agreements exempt. However Defendants may potentially argue that by using the phrase credit agreement rather than regulated agreement, as used elsewhere in the statute, Parliament intends section 140A to apply to all credit agreements regardless of whether they are regulated or exempt.

The consequence if this argument succeeds is also unclear. *Dimond*, as noted above, only covered the situation where the agreement was automatically unenforceable. Claimants can argue that it just does not matter if an agreement is potentially unenforceable. According to section 140B(2) it is for the Claimant, as the debtor, to challenge the fairness of the relationship. The Defendant cannot force to the Claimant to take this challenge; after all, the Claimant is not obliged to enter uncertain litigation in order to mitigate their loss. Defendants can argue that Judges should determine for themselves whether the relationship is unfair and what the consequence is. Agreements cannot be half unfair: they are either fair or unfair and it only waits for the Court to determine which. Defendants running this argument may wish to consider whether to join the hire company as a party to the proceedings.

These arguments have never been tested in the Courts.

C) UNFAIR TERMS IN CONSUMER CONTRACTS REGULATIONS 1999

Unfair contract terms arguments have never featured regularly in credit hire cases. However, it might be possible for Defendants to argue that exemption clauses are unfair contract terms and thus are not binding.[6] After all, such clauses are designed to oust consumer protection legislation and therefore limit the rights of the consumer.

The Unfair Terms in Consumer Contracts Regulations 1999 came into force on 1 October 1999. The intention of the Regulations was to prevent "unfair" terms in contracts with a consumer from binding the consumer.

When considering the potential role of the 1999 Regulations, there are essentially two questions: do the fairness provisions of the 1999 Regulations apply to the term in question and is the term unfair?

---

6   In making this argument, the Defendant's ultimate goal is to persuade the Court that the agreement is regulated by the Consumer Credit Act and as a result unenforceable.

Application of the Fairness Provisions in the 1999 Regulations

The 1999 Regulations apply to "unfair terms in contracts concluded between a seller or a supplier and a consumer" (Regulation 4(1)). Regulation 3(1) defines both "supplier" and "consumer". There is no doubt that a credit hire company is a supplier within the meaning of the Regulations. The definition of consumer is: "any natural person who, in contracts covered by these Regulations, is acting for purposes which are outside his trade, business or profession." Thus the Regulations only protect natural persons: a company which hires a vehicle, even if it acts for purposes outside its business, cannot rely on the Regulations.[7]

The Regulations only apply to terms which have not been individually negotiated (cf Regulation 5(1)). The burden of proof is on the supplier to show that a term was individually negotiated (Regulation 5(4)). However, this is likely to cover most credit hire agreements because they are standard form agreements.

Certain terms in contracts are exempt from scrutiny under the 1999 Regulations. Regulation 4(2) provides that:

> *"these Regulations do not apply to contractual terms which reflect (a) mandatory statutory or regulatory provisions…"*

Claimants may argue that an exemption clause reflects statutory provisions. Interestingly, the wording of Regulation 4(2)(a) had been amended since the 1994 Regulations to add the word "mandatory", which also appeared in Council Directive 93/13 on which the Regulations were modelled. This is significant because whilst an exemption clause may reflect statutory provisions, they do not reflect a "mandatory statutory…provision".

Further, Regulation 6(2) provides that:

> *"in so far as it is in plain intelligibly language, the assessment of fairness of a term shall not relate:*

---

7   See the discussion of the definition of consumer in early chapters.

a) to the definition of the main subject matter of the contract, or
b) to the adequacy of the price or remuneration, as against the
goods or services supplied in exchange."

This is generally thought to exclude the core terms of the contract from the requirement of fairness. The reason is that the 1999 Regulations are not a mechanism of price control or indeed quality control. They are not intended to undermine the parties' freedom to contract. Thus the courts must distinguish between those terms which express the substance of the bargain and those other incidental terms which surround them.

In *Director General of Fair Trading v First National Bank Plc,*[8] the House of Lords took a restrictive interpretation of which terms count as core terms. Lord Bingham held that:

"The object of the Regulations and the Directive is to protect con-
sumers against the inclusion of unfair and prejudicial terms in
standard-form contracts into which they enter, and that object
would plainly be frustrated if regulation 3(2)(b) were so broadly
interpreted as to cover any terms other than those falling squarely
within it."[9]

This suggests that Claimants are likely to find it difficult to argue that a term challenged by the Defendants falls within Regulation 6(2). Nevertheless Regulation 6(2) would appear to prevent Defendants from arguing that the rate of hire was itself unfair. The rate of hire is likely to be regarded as a core term.

Is the Term Unfair?

Regulation 5(1) provides that *"a contractual term which has not been indi-*
vidually negotiated shall be regarded as unfair if, contrary to the requirement

---

8   [2002] 1 AC 481. Although this case in fact related to the 1994 Regulations, it is submitted that the reasoning of the House of Lords remains relevant to the 1999 Regulations.

9   *Ibid.*, para. 12.

of good faith, it causes a significant imbalance in the parties' rights and obligations arising under the contract, to the detriment of the consumer".

Regulation 6(1) states that all the circumstances surrounding the contract must be taken into account when assessing whether a term is fair. In particular the courts are enjoined to consider the nature of the good or services concerned and the circumstances attending the conclusion of the contract.

Regard should also be had to Schedule 2, which lays down an *"indicative and non-exhaustive list of terms which may be regarded as unfair"*. One example of this is a term which irrevocably binds the consumer to a term with which he had no real opportunity of becoming acquainted before the conclusion of the contract (schedule 2(1)(i) of the Regulations).

In *Director General of Fair Trading v First National Bank Plc* the House of Lords considered the meaning of the test for unfairness for the first time. It is worth setting out some passages from their speeches:

> *"The requirement of significant imbalance is met if a term is so weighted in favour of the supplier as to tilt the parties' rights and obligations under the contract significantly in his favour. This may be by the granting to the supplier of a beneficial option or discretion or power, or by the imposing on the consumer of a disadvantageous burden or risk or duty...*
>
> *The requirement of good faith in this context is one of fair and open dealing. Openness requires that the terms should be expressed fully, clearly and legibly, containing no concealed pitfalls or traps. Appropriate prominence should be given to terms which might operate disadvantageously to the customer. Fair dealing requires that a supplier should not, whether deliberately or unconsciously, take advantage of the consumer's necessity, indigence, lack of experience, unfamiliarity with the subject matter of the contract, weak bargaining position or any other factor listed in or analogous to those listed in Schedule 2 to the Regulations."*[10]

---

10 *Ibid.*, per Lord Bingham at para. 17.

"There can be no one single test of this [unfairness]. It is obviously useful to assess the impact of an impugned term on the parties' rights and obligations by comparing the effect of the contract with the term and the effect it would have without it. But the inquiry cannot stop there. It may also be necessary to consider the effect of the inclusion of the term on the substance or core of the transaction; whether if it were drawn to his attention the consumer would be likely to be surprised by it; whether the term is a standard term, not merely in similar non-negotiable consumer contracts, but in commercial contracts freely negotiated between parties acting on level terms and at arms' length; and whether, in such cases, the party adversely affected by the inclusion of the term or his lawyer might reasonably be expected to object to its inclusion and press for its deletion. The list is not necessarily exhaustive; other approaches may sometimes be more appropriate."[11]

Ultimately the question of whether or not a term is unfair is dependent on all the facts and circumstances of an individual case.

The Effect of a Clause being held to be "Unfair"

If a clause is found to be unfair it does not bind the consumer (Regulation 8(1)). Thus if the Defendant successfully argued that a term exempting a contract from Consumer Credit legislation was unfair, the Defendant could go on to argue that the provisions of the Consumer Credit Act ought to apply in the normal way. This may lead to the contract being unenforceable. However, note that the fact that the clause does not bind the consumer is not the same as rendering it void or unenforceable. Individual Claimants in credit hire cases may well argue that while the term does not bind the Claimant himself, this finding should have no effect on the Defendant's liability.

To pursue such an attack, the Defendant is likely to need to join the credit hire company into the litigation to determine the specific issue of unfairness.

---

11 *Ibid.*, per Lord Millett at para 54.

D) **SIGNATURE OF THE HIRE AGREEMENT**

i) No Signature

If there is no signed hire agreement, then questions naturally arise as to whether the contract was properly formed. In particular, the Defendant may be able to argue that the Claimant never actually agreed to hire a vehicle, never intended to enter legal relations with the hire company or entered into an unenforceable oral consumer credit agreement.

Claimants should not lose sight of the practical difficulties inherent in such cases. Courts are used to seeing standard form signed agreements. In the absence of such basic documentation, the Courts are unlikely to be well disposed to the Claim. It follows that if there is no signed agreement, Claimants would do well to anticipate the potential difficulty and explain the nature of any oral agreement in the witness statements.

Nevertheless, the absence of a signature need not be decisive. In considering a late signature case, HHJ Freedman observed that the conclusion below that there was never an agreement was *"astonishing"* because *"looking at the matter in its commercial context [...] it is inconceivable, in my judgment, that any hire company would allow a vehicle to be kept and used by a hirer [...] in excess of three weeks without having any contractual protection in force"*.[12] In many cases, commercial common sense will be a powerful argument against the conclusion that there was in reality no contract. HHJ Freedman later added *"it is not necessary to cite authority for the proposition that there can be a contract in place without a signature appearing on a document"*.[13]

Claimants may also consider arguing that absence of an agreement is not fatal to the claim. They might argue by analogy with *Bee v Jenson* that they can still advance a claim for general damages for loss of use, in the same sum as the hire charges. Additionally, Claimants might argue that they remain vulnerable to claim from the hire company founded in restitution.

---

12 *Armstrong v Hussain*, Newcastle County Court, unreported, 29 May 2015 at para. 9.

13 *Ibid.*, para. 18.

ii) Late Signature

A different situation arises where the Claimant did not sign the hire agreement at the time, but did sign it at a later date. Here Defendants have argued that there was no consideration for entering into the written hire agreement, because past consideration is no consideration, and hence the written agreement is invalid.

I n *Carson v Tazaki Foods Ltd,*[14] the Claimant spoke with the hire company on the telephone. She then received a hire car for three days. The hire documents were sent to her in the post at the time of hire, but she did not actually sign the papers until months later. It was held that the Claimant entered into a contract with the hire company orally by telephone and that the terms of that contract were identical to the subsequent written terms. The best evidence of the terms of agreement was the signed written documents, even where that signature was late. Hence there was an enforceable agreement.

A similar though not identical result was reached in *Borley v Reed,*[15] in which the Court held that during the preliminary telephone call, the Claimant agreed to use the hire company subject to the detailed terms and conditions which would be sent to her later. As a result, the content of the telephone call did not constitute a concluded oral agreement. The Court described this arrangement as commonplace. Again this constituted an enforceable agreement.

In both cases, the Courts expressed concern about the viability of the Defendant's arguments. Thus in *Borley v Reed*, the Judge said *"I do not understand why the law should contemplate with equanimity the determined attempt on the part of the tortfeasor's insurers to meddle in that sensible and beneficial arrangement [the hire agreement]"*. In *Carson v Tazaki Foods Ltd*, whilst the Judge accepted that close analysis of contract was a feature of credit hire litigation, he went on to comment that the evidential burden on the Claimant would be light in such cases and

---

14 Central London County Court, HHJ Mackie QC, unreported, 25 August 2005.
15 HHJ Hughes QC, unreported, 20 October 2005.

it would be very difficult for Defendants to succeed on such points. Defendants should therefore be cautious about such arguments.

To those cases, we should now add *Armstrong v Hussain* in which HHJ Freedman found that after an initial telephone conversation with his Solicitor, a hire car and the terms and conditions were delivered to the Claimant. He delayed in signing and returning them, until the day after the hire period ended. The Court held that "once he has the terms and conditions and he is not taking exception to them and he continues to keep and drive the car, then on any view of the matter, there is a concluded agreement and it matters not that he does not sign the agreement until a day after the hire period".[16]

That said, the Defendant succeeded on a similar argument in *Company Call Centre Technology Ltd v Sheehan*.[17] In that case the Claimant company hired a replacement vehicle from 19 March 2007 to 3 April 2007. The hire agreement was signed by a representative of the company on 12 August 2007, and the oral evidence suggested that the written agreement was only received by the company shortly before it was signed. In those circumstances, on appeal the Court refused to accept that the trial Judge was wrong to find that there was no agreement to pay the hire charges.

There were two factual distinctions which go some way towards explaining the result in this case. First, there was no evidence about an initial oral discussion between Claimant and hire company.[18] Second, unlike in *Carson* and *Armstrong*, there was no evidence that the Claimant had the terms and conditions available to it whilst the hire was ongoing. That is significant because the Claimant would not therefore be aware of the contractual terms until after the hire vehicle had been returned.

---

16 Armstrong v Hussain, para. 17.

17 HHJ Worster, unreported, 26 February 2009.

18 This highlights the importance of putting forwards the best evidence. Given that the Claimant was a company it may be that there was an earlier oral agreement, but that the witness (who later signed the written agreement) was not able to speak to it.

However, we also note that on appeal the Court in *Company Call Centre* did not have to deal with issues of novation or of restitution, since those were not raised at all at first instance. This suggests that even where the facts are closer to *Company Call Centre* than to *Carson* and *Borley*, the Claimant should be prepared to argue that there remains a claim in restitution or founded in novation.

iii) Signed by a different person

A situation which frequently arises in the County Courts is that the hire agreement turns out to have been signed by a different person from the owner of the damaged vehicle and / or the named Claimant. It is not uncommon for cases to be dismissed on the basis that the claim should have been brought by the signatory / the owner.

Nevertheless, it is suggested that cases should not automatically be dismissed on this basis. Rather it depends on the evidence about the formation of the agreement. In very many of these cases, the person who signed the agreement is a family member, who has been specifically instructed by the Claimant to sign the agreement on the Claimant's behalf. This often happens where, for example, the hire car has to be delivered whilst the Claimant is out at work. In these circumstances, the Claimant can readily argue that the agreement was signed on his authority by a family member acting as his agent.

Again, where this is likely to be an issue, the Claimant would do well to anticipate the problem and address it in witness statements. In the absence of proper evidence, it is more difficult for the Court to conclude that there was an agency arrangement in place.

iv) Bailment

A related issue arises from the law of bailment. Suppose an individual lawfully borrows a friend's car and has a no-fault accident in it. Can that individual bring a claim for the cost of hire charges (and indeed repair charges), or must the claim for hire charges be brought by the owner of the car?

Although the early shipping cases were not entirely clear on the point, the present position is that the bailee of property can sue in tort in respect of damage to the bailed goods.[19] This left only the question whether the bailee could sue in respect of the bailor's loss of use or only for repairs and his personal loss of use. In *Richards v Thomas*[20] HHJ Price QC held that the bailee can recover "all losses arising from damage to a chattel whilst in his hands". A claim for hire charges by the bailee was therefore allowed.

Assuming that this approach is correct in principle, it nevertheless creates certain practical problems. First, if the bailee is effectively claiming loss of use on behalf of the owner – and especially if the hire agreement was signed by the owner, then evidence about need, impecuniosity and mitigation should presumably relate to the owner. Claimants would need to ensure that that evidence is available. If the bailee is left to attempt to answer questions about the owner's need and financial position, the result is likely to be unedifying.

A number of the above issues were discussed in *Mungall v West Oxfordshire District Council*.[21] That was a case in which the damaged vehicle was leased to a company. The director of the company gave the vehicle to his son to use, although his son had no other connection to the company and paid nothing for it. The father entered into a credit hire agreement, signed by the son as his agent, but the use of the hired vehicle was exclusively the son's. Both had sought to recover the hire charges at first instance.

HHJ Harris QC put the problem pithily: the father had no need for a replacement vehicle (he had not lost the use of the damaged vehicle which he had not owned, leased or driven). The son did lose the use of the vehicle, but he was not responsible for the hire charges and hence before and after the accident he remained "the happy recipient of a free car".[22]

---

19 *O'Sullivan v Williams* [1992] 3 All ER 385, relying on *the Winkfield* (1902) Probate 42.

20 [1997] CLY 1777.

21 Oxford County Court, HHJ Harris QC, 3 November 2014.

22 *Ibid.*, para. 4.

The Court held that the son could not claim as special damages the money spent on a replacement car which he had not paid or contracted to pay.[23] In reliance on *Bee v Jensen*, however, the son, as the regular driver of the vehicle, did have a claim for general damages for loss of use and that claim could be measured by the reasonable cost of hiring a replacement vehicle.[24]

Although the Claimants succeeded in *Mungall*, the case exposes the analytical difficulties which can arise in pursuing such a claim. As a result, hire companies may observe that this case would have been more straightforward had the credit hire agreement been made with the son himself or, perhaps, with the company. The complications only arose because the credit hire agreement was with the father, who was the person with the least interest in the vehicle on the facts.

HHJ Harris QC raised in passing a further potential difficulty – whether a negligent driver who damages another vehicle actually owes a duty of care to someone who is not the owner of the other vehicle but who has use of that vehicle.[25] He described the issue as "potentially complex" and it presumably turns on the limits of duty of care according to the well-known principles in cases like *Caparo v Dickman*.[26] But, at least in cases where the primary user of the vehicle happens not to be the owner, it is thought that no issue should arise; there would be a significant gap in the law if such a person was left without a remedy.

E) <u>ORAL ASSURANCES / REPRESENTATIONS</u>
1

One of the most common issues which can arise from cross-examination of the claimant, is that the claimant suggests that they were told that they would never have to pay for the hire car or, at least, that no payment will be due until after the litigation has come to an end (which may be longer than the prescribed twelve months for consumer credit purposes). What legal effect might these assurances have?

---

23 *Ibid.*, para. 19.
24 *Ibid.*, para. 22.
25 *Ibid.*, para. 16.
26 [1990] 2 WLR 358.

The starting point is that where the Claimant has signed a written hire agreement, he is likely to be bound by what he signed. As a matter of contract law, oral assurances would not ordinarily be relevant pursuant to the 'parol evidence rule'. However, there have been a number of modern cases which have whittled away at the parol evidence rule on various grounds. Oral assurances may be relied on in support of the arguments set out below.

Collateral contracts

Depending on the facts, it may also be argued that the main credit hire agreement was entered into by the Claimant only in consideration of a promise by the credit hire company that they would never enforce the agreement against him. In such a case, it could be argued that a collateral contract has arisen. Therefore, the Claimant cannot rely on a term in the main contract suggesting that he has a liability if it is contradicted by a term in the collateral contract suggesting that in reality he does not.[27]

Against this, Claimants and credit hire companies may argue that there was never any legal intention to enter into a collateral contract. Further, credit hire companies may claim that any such suggestion was mere sales talk and did not amount to a legal representation. Finally, it should be noted that in at least one of the cases in *Giles v Thompson*, publicity materials had suggested that the car would be free but this did not lead the Court to dismiss the claim.[28]

Estoppel

The oral assurance may create an estoppel preventing the hire company from relying on provisions which contradict it.[29] However, estoppel is

---

27 See cases such as *City and Westminster Properties (1934) Ltd v Mudd* [1959] 1 Ch 129 and Lord Denning MR in *J. Evans & Son (Portsmouth) Limited v Andrea Merzario Limited* (above).

28 [1993] 3 All ER 321, 364H–365B. However Lord Mustill did suggest that this practice should be changed.

29 See *City and Westminster Properties* (1934) Ltd.

usually thought of as a shield rather than a sword: the Claimant could use estoppel to defend a claim brought by the hire company but could not base a claim on it. This limits the usefulness of estoppel to Defendant insurers, though estoppel may well be relevant should a hire company ever try to enforce the agreement against a Claimant.

Misrepresentation

The oral assurance may amount to a misrepresentation making the con-tract voidable.[30]

This is likely to be hard to prove since the Defendant would need to establish that a positive misrepresentation was made (as opposed to mere sales talk) and that this induced the Claimant to enter into the contract.[31]

In any event, Claimants may argue that the effect of a misrepresentative is that the agreement is voidable and not void. It therefore remains enforceable by a Court, until the Claimant elects to void it. A liability therefore remains for which it can be argued the Claimant should be com-pensated by the Defendant. Defendants may say that in any event, a failure to rescind the contract would be a failure to mitigate, though this argument is likely to weak because (as set out above) a Claimant does not have to take the risk of uncertain litigation against a third party[32] nor the risk of being sued by a third party.

---

30 See *L'Estrange v Graucob* [1934] 2 KB 394, *Couchman v Hill* [1947] 1 KB 554, *Thomas Witter Limited v TBP Industries Limited* [1996] 2 All ER 573, *Bleakley v Grimway* [1998] 2 CL 125, *Rendle v Hicks* [1998] 2 CL 126 and *Pinder v Martin* [1998] 11 CL 160. See also the case of *County NatWest Bank Ltd v Barton and Others* [1999] Times, 29 July (on fraudulent misrepresentation) and the case of *EA Grimstead & Son Limited v McGarrigan*, Court of Appeal, [1999] Lawtel 27 October (in the context of entire agreement clauses).

31 It is worth recalling again that in *Giles v Thompson* the suggestion in publicity that the hire car was free did not prevent the Claimant recovering.

32 See *McGregor on Damages* at paragraph 327, citing the dictum of Harman J in *Pilkington v Wood* [1953] Ch. 770 that, "the so-called duty to mitigate does not go so far as to oblige the injured party, even under an indemnity, to embark on a complicated and difficult piece of litigation against a third party".

"Entire agreement" clauses

In this context, it is worth noting that many standard form credit hire agreements contain entire agreement clauses. These are clauses which state that the written agreement contains the whole agreement between the parties, and neither party will rely on any earlier oral representations.

The usual effect of such a clause is to prevent any party from relying on earlier oral representations in any subsequent litigation.[33] As a result, a properly drafted entire agreement clause takes the sting out of any argument based on an oral representation. However, Defendants may argue, depending upon the facts, that the entire agreement clause is unfair pursuant to the Unfair Terms Regulations or indicative of an Unfair Relationship

F) **MINORS**

Where the Claimant is a minor,[34] the Defendant may argue that a hire agreement is not enforceable against him. For obvious reasons, it is relatively rare to find persons under the age of 18 hiring vehicles but the issue can arise in the context of low powered mopeds or similar vehicles.

Subject to exceptions, the only contracts which are generally binding on a minor are "contracts for necessaries",[35] other contracts in general being voidable unless or until the minor ratifies them after attaining the age of majority.

It is unclear whether a credit hire contract is a contract for necessaries. The concept of "necessaries" appears to stretch beyond the obvious needs for food, shelter and medicine to matters which have a real use beyond the

---

33 There is a detailed discussion of the point in *EA Grimstead & Son Ltd v McGarrigan.*

34 18 is the age of capacity pursuant to the Family Law Reform Act 1969 section 1.

35 Aside from agreements related to apprenticeships or education

ornamental or the convenient.[36] Thus Claimants may argue that wherever the Claimant is able to demonstrate need for a hire vehicle, the agreement is a contract for necessaries. Defendants may argue that the standard required in this context is more exacting, in order to protect the minor.

Plainly, the facts are likely to be significant. If a vehicle is required in order to travel to employment, apprenticeship or education, then the Claimant's position is strengthened.

Even if the hire agreement is not a contract for necessaries, it may still become binding on the Claimant if it is expressly or impliedly ratified once he reaches the age of majority.[37] Issuing proceedings against the Defendant might be construed as ratification of the credit hire agreement, provided of course that the Claimant is over eighteen. As above, the Defendant might argue that ratification in these circumstances would amount to a failure to mitigate.

G) <u>ILLEGALITY</u>

Where the Claimant did not have insurance on his own vehicle, the Defendant may argue that a claim for credit hire charges should not be allowed as a matter of public policy.

In *Hewison v Meridien Shipping PTE,*[38] the Claimant claimed damages for personal injury including a substantial claim for future loss of earnings. He was employed as a crane operator. He was epileptic. He had not disclosed his epilepsy to his employer: such disclosure would have prevented him working in this capacity.

After a detailed review of the authorities, the majority of the Court of Appeal concluded that "where a claimant has to rely upon his or her own unlawful act in order to establish the whole or part of his or her claim the claim will fail either wholly or in part".[39]

---

36 See Chitty on Contracts, 8-008 and examples given at 8-016
37 See Chitty on Contracts. 8-043 - 8-045
38 [2002] EWCA civ 1821.
39 *Ibid.*, para. 29.

However, where the illegality is purely "collateral" or "insignificant"[40] the Claimant can still recover. It is for this reason that Claimants can recover loss of earnings even where they did not pay tax or national insurance on their pre-accident earnings.[41]

On the facts of *Hewison*, the majority went on to hold that in order to prove his claim for future loss of earnings, the Claimant had to assert that he would have continued in his job but for the accident. In order to keep working in that capacity he would have had to continue to deceive his employer. In so doing he would commit the criminal offence of obtaining a pecuniary advantage by deception. Accordingly his claim for loss of earnings was dismissed.[42]

Hewison was applied in the credit hire context in *Agheampong v Allied Manufacturing (London) Ltd.*[43] In that case, the Claimant was not insured to drive his own vehicle. Accordingly the Defendant argued that the claim for hire charges, as a claim for loss of use, was based on the assertion that but for the accident the Claimant would have continued to use his own vehicle. Continued use of his own vehicle was unlawful because it was not insured. Hence, the Defendant argued that the claim for hire charges should be dismissed.

It is noteworthy that there is a distinction between these cases and *Hewison*, because in these cases it is open to the Claimant to insure his own vehicle at any time. Thus the Court accepted in *Agheampong* that in order to succeed on the evidence, the Defendant must establish that the Claimant would have continued to drive his own car without insurance throughout the hire period.[44]

---

40 *Ibid.,* para. 36, 43.

41 See *Newman v Fowkes* [2002] EWCA Civ 519.

42 *Hewison*, para 45. Note that the majority thought the result would have been different had the deception not been deliberate.

43 HHJ Dean QC, unreported, 30 June 2008.

44 *Ibid.,* para. 85.

The burden of proof rests on the Defendant. It was accepted in *Agheampong* that given that the allegation is of criminal conduct, a "heightened" standard of proof applied. That is whilst the standard of proof remained the balance of probabilities, "more cogent evidence" was required to cross that threshold.[45]

On the facts of *Agheampong*, the Defendant was able to meet that burden of proof. The Court concluded that the Claimant had deliberately misled the Court about his historical insurance position.[46] He had driven without insurance for around 16 months, and given his "general behaviour" and "devious attempt to explain it away" the Court was satisfied that he would have continued to drive without insurance in the future.[47]

The Court concluded that the Claimant did have to rely on this illegality in order to establish his claim for loss of use. Taking into account the losses caused by uninsured motorists, the length of time without insurance and the fact that the Claimant was also driving without paying road tax, the illegality was not insignificant. The case therefore "falls squarely within" the principle identified in *Hewison*.[48] The claim for hire charges was dismissed.

This is potentially a significant decision for Defendants, because it is a clear application of the principles in *Hewison* to the credit hire context. The principles involved might apply wherever it is illegal for the Claimant to drive his own vehicle (ie where road tax has lapsed perhaps, or where it is technically unroadworthy prior to the accident).

Defendants may also argue that illegality is fatal to the claim for hire charges where the hire vehicle turns out not to be insured. However, it should be noted that this conclusion does not necessarily follow from *Hewison* and *Agheampong*. In such a situation, the claim for loss of use is not founded on illegality, because the Claimant does not need to rely on

---

45 *Ibid.*, para. 86 – 87.
46 *Ibid.*, para. 112.
47 *Ibid.*, para. 116.
48 *Ibid.*, para. 137.

unlawful conduct in order to found a claim for loss of use. This issue therefore remains open to argument.

Further, Claimants may note that the facts of *Agheampong* were relatively extreme in that the claimant in that case had been driving without insurance for a substantial period of time and this enabled the Court to infer that he would have continued to do so. Where insurance has only just lapsed, the Claimant may argue that the illegality is insignificant or that he made a simple mistake which he would have remedied shortly.

In any event, we note that the law on illegality is a hot topic at the moment. Since the last edition of this book, the Supreme Court or Court of Appeal have considered defences relying broadly on illegality in the following cases:-

(a) *Patel v Mirza*, a claim in unjust enrichment was not necessarily prevented where the claimant was seeking to recover money paid pursuant to a contract to carry out an unlawful activity;[49]

(b) *Beaumont v Ferrer*, injured claimant precluded from claiming damages from defendant taxi driver, in circumstances where he was trying to run from the taxi without paying;[50]

(c) *Les Laboratoires Serveir v Apotex Inc,* in the circumstances of the case illegality did not bar a claim on a cross-undertaking in damages in patent infringement proceedings;[51]

(d) *Hounga v Allen*, an illegal immigrant who worked for the defendant pursuant to an unlawful contract of employment, could claim unlawful discrimination as a result of serious abuse at the defendants' hand.[52]

---

49 [2016] UKSC 42.
50 [2016] EWCA civ 768.
51 [2014] UKSC 55.
52 [2014] UKSC 47.

Through these and other cases, issues arising out of defences of illegality have come before the highest courts in a variety of different contexts an unusual number of times in the past three years. As a result, the law is currently in a state of flux. Many of the cases feature dissenting or partially dissenting speeches. It would therefore be unwise to draw any firm conclusions at this stage.

Nevertheless, it appears to be the case that the Courts are moving towards emphasising the importance of the underlying public policy in assessing the defence of illegality. Although criticised for tending towards uncertainty, that approach necessarily involves considering a range of factors including the link between the illegality and the claim and the seriousness of the illegality. It remains to be seen how these considerations would apply in a credit hire context. There is ample scope for argument. Claimants may argue, for instance that the public policy behind the offence of driving without insurance is to ensure that in the event of an accident, the innocent party is able to recovery compensation; that public policy does not necessarily require that an uninsured driver is unable to recover credit hire charges. The reasoning in *Agheampong* and indeed in *Hewison* will likely need to be reconsidered in the light of the developing authorities on illegality.

CHAPTER EIGHT
MISCELLANEOUS

A. <u>INTRODUCTION</u>

The purpose of this chapter is to address a range of other issues which the practitioner will frequently encounter in dealing with credit hire claims, including procedural issues, claims for interest on credit hire charges and claims for engineer's fees. Further, the chapter concludes with a section summarising the law on champerty, which was the Insurers' first big challenge to the credit hire industry but which is now only of historical interest.

B. <u>PROCEDURAL ISSUES</u>

The Pre-Action Protocol

We will not rehearse all the civil procedure rules or pre-action protocols here. Nevertheless, the relatively recent introduction and expansion of the Pre-action Protocol for Low Value Personal Injury Claims in Road Traffic Accidents presents a number of additional opportunities and issues.

The first question is whether a credit hire claim should be submitted through the Protocol. The Protocol applies, as its name suggests, to claims which include a claim for personal injury.[1] Where there is no personal injury claim, there is no need to abide by the Protocol. Where there is both a personal injury claim and a credit hire claim, the position is less clear. The Protocol provides that a claim "may include" vehicle related damages (which include credit hire charges) but that "these are excluded for the purposes of valuing the claim".[2] Further, a later paragraph suggests that "Claims for vehicle related damages will ordinarily be dealt with outside the provisions of this Protocol under industry agreements".[3] The result is that the Claimant can choose to include a credit hire claim of any value within a Protocol claim, although the presumption appears to be that they will be left out of the Protocol.

Claimants should be aware that in certain circumstances they may face difficulties if a credit hire claim is not included in a Protocol claim. First, the Protocol provides that where the original claim has not settled and there remain additional vehicle related damages being dealt with by a third party separate from the claim, "the claimant must in relation to the additional damages (1) notify the defendant that this separate claim is being considered [...] (3) make a separate offer".[4] This appears to require a claimant claiming personal injury to ensure that the defendant is notified of the credit hire claim before settling the personal injury claim. Second, the Claims Notification Form which starts the Protocol process contains questions requiring the Claimant to indicate whether he is in a hire vehicle. In *Smikle v Global Logistics*,[5] the Claimant had indicated that on the Claims Notification Form that there was no claim for hire charges. His personal injury claim settled. Subsequently, he issued proceedings with a different Solicitor claiming credit hire charges. His claim was struck out as an abuse of process on the basis that the Defendant was entitled to rely on the indication in the CNF that there was no claim for hire charges. Since it is not uncommon for different solicitors to represent the claimant in respect of credit hire charges and per-

---

1 Para. 4.1 of the Pre-Action Protocol.

2 *Ibid.,* para. 4.4.

3 Ibid., para. 7.23.

4 *Ibid.,* para. 7.52.

5 Walsall County Court, DJ McQueen, 3 June 2016.

sonal injuries, there is potential for Defendants to take these points more often.

Important consequences also follow from including the credit hire claim within the Protocol. First, the Protocol sets out a rigid procedure moving through fixed stages designed to resolve cases at relatively low cost. Ultimately, at Stage 3 they move to Court through Part 8 proceedings. If a hearing is required, the Court will consider written evidence only. This means that the Court will have to resolve the credit hire claim on limited evidence in limited time. The Court can only re-allocate the Claim to Part 7 if "(1) further evidence must be provided by any party; and (2) the claim is not suitable to continue under the Stage 3 procedure". In *Phillips v Willis*, the Court of Appeal held that these conditions were not satisfied in relation to a credit hire claim in which the sums in dispute were low and the additional evidence which might be required appeared limited.[6] The claim should therefore have been decided under the Stage 3 procedure. The Court added that the case could have transferred if it involved "very high hire charges" or "complex issues of law and fact".[7] Since detailed scrutiny of the hire charges and oral evidence may benefit the Defendant, it may assist Claimants to take advantage of the relatively limited scrutiny afforded by the Protocol procedures wherever possible.

Second, where a claim is started under the Protocol but does not continue under the Protocol and Part 7 proceedings are issued, the fixed costs regime set out in CPR 45.29A – L will apply. The costs regime is restrictive; where a claim resolves at trial, profit costs allowed are £2,655 plus 20% of damages. This might encourage Claimants to issue credit hire claims separately. However, one issue that remains open to Defendants to argue is that fixed costs should apply where a personal injury claim is started through the Protocol but the Claimant elects to issue a claim for credit hire charges separately – so potentially obtaining two sets of costs.

---

6   [2016] EWCA Civ 401.

7   *Ibid.*, para. 35.

Qualified One Way Costs Shifting

Where a claim includes a claim for damages for personal injury, the claimant is now protected against the defendant's costs by qualified one way costs shifting. These rules do not apply to credit hire claims which do not include a personal injury claim.

Where both personal injuries and credit hire are claimed, we draw attention to CPR 44.16(2) which provides that "Orders for costs made against the claimant may be enforced up to the full extent of such orders with the permission of the court, and to the extent it considers just, where – (a) the proceedings include a claim which is made for the financial benefit of a person other than the claimant...."

The Practice Direction to Part 44 adds at paragraph 12.2 that "examples of claims made for the financial benefit of someone other than the claimant [...] are subrogated claims and claims for credit hire".

Further paragraph 12.5 provides that:

> *"In a case to which rule 44.16(2)(a) applies (claims for the benefit of others:-*
> *a) The court will usually order any person other than the claimant for whose benefit such a claim was made to pay all the costs of the proceedings or the costs attributable to the issues to which rule 44.16(2)(a) applies, or may exceptionally make an order permitting the enforcement of such costs against the claimant;*
> *b) The court may, as it thinks fair and just, determine the costs attributable to claims for the financial benefit of persons other than the claimant"*

Thus, where the claim fails, the effect of the Practice Direction is clearly that the Court may order the credit hire company to pay all of the Defendant's costs or those costs attributable to the credit hire charges.

Claimants may challenge whether this is really what CPR 44.16(2)(a) means. Is the Practice Direction correct that a claim for credit hire charges is a claim "for the financial benefit of someone other than the claimant". A significant number of special damages concern items that the Claimant would effectively pay over to a third party – for instance physiotherapy charges. It is unclear why credit hire charges should be singled out – after all, if the Claimant does not pay them, he or she is left with a contractual liability to pay the hire company and therefore paying them is for his financial benefit. However, Defendants may respond that the wording of the Practice Direction is clear and the legislative intention was to exempt credit hire claims for the protection of qualified one way costs shifting.

Allocation

It is well known that claims worth less than £10,000 are normally allocated to the small claims track and claims worth more than £10,000 but less than £25,000 to the fast track. However, in credit hire claims, an option open to the Defendant is to admit part of the claim for credit hire charges and so bring the amount in dispute within the small claims track. In *Akhtar v Boland*,[8] the Court of Appeal confirmed that where an unqualfied admission of part of the hire charges is made, leaving the amount in dispute below £10,000, the claim will ordinarily be allocated to the small claims track. Of course, this is usually beneficial to the Defendant because it limits the amount of costs recoverable.

However, Defendants should be aware of two related problems. The first is that the Claimant is entitled to enter judgment on the admission and to continue to claim the remainder of the hire charges. Having made a partial but unqualified admission, the Defendant is likely to find that any allegations inconsistent with that admission will be disregarded. It may follow, as in *Akhtar*, that "the defendant could not, for example, challenge the entitlement of the claimant to damages for loss of use of his vehicle, or the reasonable need of the claimant to hire a replacement vehicle for a reasonable time and at a reasonable hire

---

8   [2014] EWCA Civ 872.

charge".[9] Thus the price that the Defendant must pay for limiting their exposure to costs, is that their ability to challenge the remaining hire charges will be limited.

Second, pursuant to the CPR PD 46 para. 7.1(3), the Court may award fast track costs up to the date when judgment was entered for the admitted sum. That may mean costs until the date of judgment, not the date that the admission was first made.[10]

C. ENGINEERS' FEES

In credit hire cases, the Claimant routinely includes a claim for the cost of an engineer assessing the damage to the Claimant's vehicle. But engineers' fees are not ordinarily recoverable. Thus, in *Burdis v Livsey* the Court of Appeal held:

> "He [the Claimant] can recover the cost of the repair unless it be shown that he has not taken reasonable steps to mitigate his loss. Of course a number of quotations or one engineer's report can be good evidence to rebut an allegation of a failure to mitigate and may be useful in settlement negotiations; but the costs are not part of the loss. The fact that insurers use engineers to report on damaged cars and agree the costs of repair is irrelevant to the assessment of the amount of loss. Helphire use an engineer to negotiate the repair charges with the repairer with no doubt the view that the engineer's report will lead to a quick and satisfactory settlement of the claim and protect Helphire. As such they would not be recoverable."[11]

In fast and multi-track cases, it remains open to Claimants to attempt to recover the hire charges as part of their costs but not as damages.

---

9   *Ibid.*, para. 21.
10 *Cameron v Office Depot (UK) Ltd*, Bromley County Court, DJ Brett, 13 July 2016.
11 Burdis v Livsey, para. 156.

Note further that where proceedings are brought simply to recover an engineer's fee, this has been held to be an abuse of the process of the court in issuing solely to recover costs (see *Warriner v Smith*[12]).

D. MISCELLANEOUS EXPENSES

Claims for the inconvenience associated with the accident and for miscellaneous expenses such as postage and telephone costs for pursuing the claim are often tagged on to a credit hire claim.

Defendants may argue that "damages for worry and for the nuisance caused by having to deal with the consequences of an accident are not recoverable."[13] Further that claims for miscellaneous expenses are claims for costs and not damages, though this is a point on which different courts take different views.[14]

E. STORAGE AND RECOVERY CHARGES

Very often a claim is made for the cost of (1) recovering the Claimant's damaged vehicle and (2) storing it until repairs can start or it can be disposed of. There is nothing wrong with such a claim in principle. However, it can be challenged on the similar grounds to the main claim for credit hire charges e.g. if there has been a deferment of the debt the Defendant may raise consumer credit arguments.

In such cases the first question is likely to be what the Claimant actually agreed to: what he contracted for, when and with whom and whether he is liable for anything on that contract. Unlike credit hire contracts, there is often no written agreement in relation to the storage charges. This means that if there is a deferment of the debt, there may well be enforceability issues.

---

12 [1999] 4 CL.

13 Per Scott VC in Dimond v Lovell.

14 *Taylor v Browne* [1995] CLY 1842 suggests that they are not recoverable, but they were recovered in *Marley v Novak* [1996] CLY 2112.

Furthermore, issues of mitigation may arise. The Defendant may argue that it was open to the Claimant to store the vehicle at his house for free. The value of the car is also relevant. It may well be argued that it is unreasonable, for example, to incur storage charges which approach or exceed the value of the vehicle.

In some cases, Claimants may be able to argue that the vehicle is being stored pending the Defendant insurer inspecting the vehicle. If this is correct then the responsibility for any delay rests with the Defendant.

F. DELIVERY AND COLLECTION CHARGES

The issue of delivery and collection charges was dealt with authoritatively in *Burdis v Livsey*. Before the Court of Appeal, all the parties agreed that these charges would sometimes be recoverable. The Court of Appeal concluded that:

> *"If injury causes damage then the injured party can recover the loss caused by the injury. But the need for a replacement car is not self-proving (see Giles v Thompson at 167 D); neither is the need for delivery self-proving. If the injured person lives next door to the car hire company, he can walk round and collect the replacement car and a delivery and collection charge is not part of the loss. However, the cost of obtaining the replacement car can be recovered subject to the duty to take reasonable steps to mitigate the loss. What is reasonable is a question of fact, which can usually be deduced from the surrounding circumstances. If there is suitable public transport, it would be reasonable to expect the car to be collected. If part of the loss is the cost of delivery and collection, that must be proved."*[15]

The result is that it is for the Claimant to prove that he needed the delivery and collection service with reference to his own specific circumstances.

---

15 *Burdis v Livsey*, para. 153.

G. INTEREST

In *Giles v Thompson*,[16] Lord Mustill said of the award of interest, *"The exercise of the right should correspond with reality"*. In that case there was no liability to pay the hire charges until judgment was given and therefore no award of interest was made.

The Court of Appeal returned to the issue in *Pattni v First Leicester Buses Ltd.*[17] In that case the Claimant argued that he was under a contractual obligation to pay interest pursuant to the hire agreement. The Court of Appeal held that contractual interest was not recoverable because it represented a charge for credit, hence an irrecoverable additional benefit.[18] In the same decision the Court of Appeal followed *Giles v Thompson* in refusing to exercise the Court's discretion to award interest.[19]

The same result was reached by HHJ Harris in *Corbett v Gaskin*.[20]

The general position is therefore that interest is not recoverable on credit hire charges. However, if insurers have already re-imbursed the credit hire company, they may be entitled to interest. Thus in *Clark v Ardington Electrical Services and others*,[21] HHJ Harris allowed interest to be awarded to a subrogated Claimant from the date of payment. He was upheld on this point in *Burdis v Livsey*.[22] The result is that if there is evidence that the hire charges have been paid (eg by an insurer so that the claim is subrogated) interest is recoverable.

---

16 [1994] AC 142 at page 168.
17 which was heard together with Bent no2: [2011] EWCA civ 1384.
18 *Ibid.*, para. 61 – 62.
19 Ibid., para. 70.
20 Unreported, 21 April 2008.
21 HHJ Harris, Oxford County Court, 14 September 2001.
22 *Ibid.*, paras. 157 – 162.

H. CHAMPERTY

Champerty consists of wrongfully interfering in the disputes of others. In *Giles v Thompson*, the Defendant insurers argued that the credit hire contracts were champertous because the credit hire companies were instigating the litigation, had a financial interest in the outcome and often were funding them. Therefore, they argued, the agreements were illegal and unenforceable against the Claimant.

In the House of Lords, Lord Mustill asked the single question whether there was:

> *"wanton and officious intermeddling with the disputes of others in where the meddler has no interest whatever, and where the assistance he render to one party or the other is without justification or excuse."*

This is essentially a question of fact. Consideration must be given to all aspects of a transaction, bearing in mind that the public policy behind the law of champerty is to *"protect the purity of justice and the interests of vulnerable litigants"*.

The House of Lords held that the credit hire agreements were not champertous. There was no realistic prospect of the administration of justice suffering. Where the Claimant retained what Steyn LJ in the Court of Appeal had termed a *"residual liability"* to pay for the hire charges, the contract would be enforceable. It was not right to say that the company was taking a share of the proceeds of litigation, rather the fruits of litigation provided a source from which the motorist could satisfy his liability to the company. This was the case if the Claimant retained a liability to pay for the hire charges whether he won or lost the case against the other side. In *Giles v Thompson* this was held to be so in all of the cases despite the fact that in at least one of them, the publicity material had suggested the cars were free.

Thus provided that the credit hire agreement imposes on the Claimant a residual liability to pay for the hire charges, the Defendant cannot rely on champerty. It is therefore no longer argued in credit hire cases.

The law of champerty has retained importance in two distinct areas of law. First, it remains a rule of professional conduct for a solicitor not to accept payment from a claimant calculated as a proportion of the sum recovered from the Defendant. Second, champerty is relevant to the assignment of bare rights of action. Broadly speaking in these two areas the court will consider whether the transaction bears the hallmarks of champerty. If it does, it is prima facie unlawful unless it can be validated by the third party having a legitimate interest in supporting the action. The law of champerty is still occasionally relied on in other contexts. Thus in *De Crittenden v Bayliss,*[23] the Court of Appeal were asked to determine whether an agreement was champertous. The Claimant and Defendant shared business interests. The Defendant was involved in litigation which, if he lost, would have damaged his financial standing and hence the Claimant's business interests. The Claimant agreed with the Defendant that he would assist him with the litigation in return for 50% of the proceeds. The two later fell out and the Claimant sued on the contract. The Defendant argued that it was champertous and hence unenforceable. But the point is no longer really relevant to credit hire litigation.

---

23 [2002] EWCA Civ 50.

MORE BOOKS BY
LAW BRIEF PUBLISHING

'A Practical Guide to Holiday Sickness Claims' by Andrew Mckie & Ian Skeate
'RTA Allegations of Fraud in a Post-Jackson Era: The Handbook, 2nd Edition' by Andrew Mckie
'RTA Personal Injury Claims: A Practical Guide Post-Jackson' by Andrew Mckie
'A Practical Guide to Personal Injuries in Sport' by Adam Walker & Patricia Leonard
'A Practical Approach to Clinical Negligence Post-Jackson' by Geoffrey Simpson-Scott
'A Practical Guide to Costs in Personal Injury Cases' by Matthew Hoe
'Occupiers, Highways and Defective Premises Claims: A Practical Guide Post-Jackson' by Andrew Mckie
'Employers' Liability Claims: A Practical Guide Post-Jackson' by Andrew Mckie
'Baby Steps: A Guide to Maternity Leave and Maternity Pay' by Leah Waller
'The Queen's Counsel Lawyer's Omnibus: 20 Years of Cartoons from the Times 1993-2013' by Alex Steuart Williams

These books and more are available to order online direct from the publisher at www.lawbriefpublishing.com, where you can also read free sample chapters. For any queries, contact us on 0844 587 2383 or mail@lawbriefpublishing.com.

Our books are also usually in stock at www.amazon.co.uk with free next day delivery for Prime members, and at good legal bookshops such as Hammicks and Wildy & Sons.

We are regularly launching new books in our series of practical day-to-day practitioners' guides. Visit our website and join our free newsletter to be kept informed.